A GROUP STUDY GUIDE

Based on the Classic Best-Seller by Henrietta Mears

New Testament

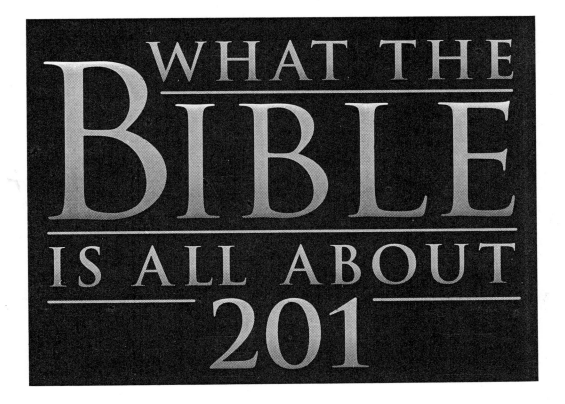

WHAT THE BIBLE IS ALL ABOUT 201

MATTHEW through PHILIPPIANS

A REPRODUCIBLE 13-SESSION BIBLE STUDY ON THE FIRST 11 BOOKS OF THE NEW TESTAMENT

Larry Keefauver, Editor

Gospel Light

Gospel Light is an evangelical Christian publisher dedicated to serving the local church. We believe God's vision for Gospel Light is to provide church leaders with biblical, user-friendly materials that will help them evangelize, disciple and minister to children, youth and families.

We hope this Gospel Light resource will help you discover biblical truth for your own life and help you minister to adults. God bless you in your work.

For a free catalog from Gospel Light please contact your Christian supplier or call 1-800-4-GOSPEL.

PUBLISHING STAFF
William T. Greig, Publisher
Dr. Elmer L. Towns, Senior Consulting Publisher
Dr. Gary S. Greig, Senior Consulting Editor
Larry Keefauver, Editor
Jean Daly, Managing Editor
Pam Weston, Editorial Assistant
Kyle Duncan, Associate Publisher
Bayard Taylor, M.Div., Editor, Theological and Biblical Issues
Debi Thayer, Designer

ISBN 0-8307-1798-6
© 1996 by Gospel Light Publications
All rights reserved.
Printed in U.S.A.

How to Make Clean Copies from This Book

You may make copies of portions of this book with a clean conscience if:
- you (or someone in your organization) are the original purchaser;
- you are using the copies you make for a noncommercial purpose (such as teaching or promoting your ministry) within your church or organization;
- you follow the instructions provided in this book.

However, it is ILLEGAL for you to make copies if:
- you are using the material to promote, advertise or sell a product or service other than for ministry fund-raising;
- you are using the material in or on a product for sale;
- you or your organization are **not** the original purchaser of this book.

By following these guidelines you help us keep our products affordable.
Thank you,
Gospel Light

CONTENTS

Contents

To complete this course in 11 *sessions* combine Sessions 9 and 10 and combine Sessions 12 and 13.

WHAT THIS COURSE IS ABOUT

God's Word is vibrant and alive, and His plan for our lives is contained between the pages of His book—the Bible. Everything we need to know about living in wholeness is contained within the pages of His Word. Yet we sometimes forget that the Bible is more than a series of unrelated, independent books—it is a connected, all-encompassing, interwoven work that provides a panoramic view of His love and plan for us.

However, the average person knows little about the Bible. Very few have a comprehensive idea of the whole book. We need, besides a microscopic study of individual books, chapters and verses, a telescopic study of God's Word in order to better understand His plan of salvation and movement in our lives. Through this study, you and your group will be able to see the interconnection between the Old and New Testaments, between the prophets and Christ. You will also see how Jesus Christ is portrayed in each book of the Bible.

The Bible is a collection of 66 books written by at least 40 authors over a period of about 1,600 years. To help us gain an accurate perspective of this monumental work, we will be using the best-selling Bible study resource *What the Bible Is All About* by Henrietta C. Mears. This book provides helpful summaries of each book of the Bible, helping us to see the common threads of good news from beginning to end.

As we begin this exploration, we must keep in mind that sometimes the Bible gives a great deal of detail, while at other times there are only brief statements. However, gaining the perspective of the Bible's major events and characters provides a helpful mental map in which to locate and understand the great riches the Book contains.

"The Bible is one book, one history, one story, His story. Behind the 10,000 events stands God, the builder of history, the maker of the ages. Eternity bounds the one side, eternity bounds the other side, and time is in between: Genesis—origins, Revelation—endings, and all the way between, God is working things out. You can go down into the minutest detail everywhere and see that there is one great purpose moving through the ages: the eternal design of the Almighty God to redeem a wrecked and ruined world" (*What the Bible Is All About* by Henrietta Mears, page 20).

In this course, *What the Bible Is All About 201 New Testament: Matthew—Philippians*, group members study the book of Matthew through the book of Philippians. God's workings and revelations are discovered while seeing how Jesus Christ is portrayed in each of these books of the Bible.

THIS GROUP STUDY GUIDE

This group study guide is a unique companion to *What the Bible Is All About*, offering a stimulating and enjoyable opportunity for group study of the whole Bible and its most important events and characters.

This group study guide is unique because it:

- Is based on the premise that a study of the Bible's most important events and characters is truly an exciting adventure of great value for everyone: novices and scholars, believers and seekers, male and female;

- Organizes the vast span of Bible history into four sections and highlights the major events and characters in each section;

- Provides useful handles for looking into the meaning of historical events, identifying the greatest fact and the greatest truth for each period of Bible history;

- Includes comprehensive One-Year and Two-Year Bible Study Plans for individual study or group study after completing the course overview;

- Requires very few additional supplies for class sessions. (An overhead projector is helpful, but not necessary. Blank paper, index cards, pencils and felt-tip pens are typical of the easily secured materials, which help add variety and stimulate involvement. Suggested supplies are listed at the beginning of each session.)

- Suggests individual reading assignments to review each session, adding further reinforcement to each person's learning.

SESSION PLAN

Each of the 13 sessions is flexibly designed to be completed in one of two time schedules:

Option A—60-minute sessions.

Option B—90-minute sessions.

You will find instructions placed in boxes and marked with the following clock symbol. This information provides optional learning experiences to extend the session to accommodate a 90-minute session.

OPTION ONE

This option will add 15 minutes to the session. These optional activities explore aspects of the main point that could not be addressed in the shorter time schedules.

OPTION TWO

This option will add 15 minutes to the session. These optional activities explore aspects of the main point that could not be addressed in the shorter time schedules.

A FEW TEACHING TIPS

1. Keep It Simple. Teaching people about the New Testament can seem like an overwhelming task. The New Testament contains a vast amount of highly interesting, deeply meaningful information. Avoid trying to pass all of this information on to your eager learners. Participants will remember far more if you keep the focus on one issue at a time, seeking to keep your explanations as brief and simple as possible.

2. Keep It Light. Some of the session introductory activities in this manual are fun! This is intentional. Many people who most need this course are intimidated by the Bible. Often there is fear that their own lack of knowledge will be exposed. People who are intimidated and fearful are not ready to learn. The light-hearted approaches are devices to help people relax so they can learn efficiently.

3. Keep It Significant. Because the course has some light touches does not mean its content can be handled frivolously. Keep clearly in mind—and repeatedly emphasize with your class—that this course is dealing with God's plan as it is revealed in the whole Bible. The insights gained in these sessions can make a big difference, not just through their increased understanding of the whole Bible, but in seeing how God's Word applies to their own lives.

4. Keep It Interactive. The learning activities in this manual provide a variety of involving experiences, recognizing the various learning styles which will be present in any group of adults. While some of the activities may not fit your preferred

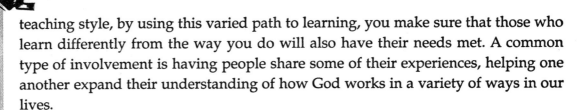

teaching style, by using this varied path to learning, you make sure that those who learn differently from the way you do will also have their needs met. A common type of involvement is having people share some of their experiences, helping one another expand their understanding of how God works in a variety of ways in our lives.

5. Keep It Prayerful. Both in your preparation and in each class session, pray earnestly that you and your class will be open to the truths of the New Testament which must be real to us if we are to enrich and deepen our relationship with God. To capture the interest of people in this course:

- Share some of your own experiences with God's Word. To succeed in leading this course, you do not need to be an expert on theology, on the Bible or on teaching methods. You do need to be honest about some of your struggles in seeking to understand and/or explain the Bible.

- Point out that while societies and cultures change, and many life experiences are different for people today than for any preceding generation, God's desire for relationship with His people has remained constant in all of human history.

- Allow people to think and talk about their own experiences with God's Word. Many adults struggle with understanding and studying the Bible, finding it difficult, an obligation that causes feelings of guilt for not achieving what they feel they are expected to. This course is not a therapy workshop, but there is great value in allowing people to be open and honest in expressing their struggles. Admission of a problem is the first step in making progress toward growth.

ALTERNATE SESSION PLANS

OPTIONS FOR USING THE FOUR *WHAT THE BIBLE IS ALL ABOUT GROUP STUDY GUIDES*

Bible Overview (Eight Sessions):

What the Bible Is All About 101 Old Testament: Genesis—Esther Session 2—Genesis to Joshua

What the Bible Is All About 101 Old Testament: Genesis—Esther Session 8—Judges to Esther

What the Bible Is All About 102 Old Testament: Job—Malachi Session 1—Job to Song of Solomon

What the Bible Is All About 102 Old Testament: Job—Malachi Session 5—Isaiah to Malachi

What the Bible Is All About 201 New Testament: Matthew—Philippians Session 1—The Four Gospels

What the Bible Is All About 201 New Testament: Matthew—Philippians Session 6—Acts to Philippians

What the Bible Is All About 202 New Testament: Colossians—Revelation Session 1—Colossians to Philemon

What the Bible Is All About 202 New Testament: Colossians—Revelation Session 8—Hebrews to Revelation

Foundations of Christianity/New Christians (13 Sessions):

What the Bible Is All About 101 Old Testament: Genesis—Esther Session 2—Genesis to Joshua

What the Bible Is All About 101 Old Testament: Genesis—Esther Session 8—Judges to Esther

What the Bible Is All About 102 Old Testament: Job—Malachi Session 1—Job to Song of Solomon

What the Bible Is All About 102 Old Testament: Job—Malachi Session 5—Isaiah to Malachi

What the Bible Is All About 201 New Testament: Matthew—Philippians Session 1—The Four Gospels

What the Bible Is All About 201 New Testament: Matthew—Philippians Session 6—Acts to Philippians

What the Bible Is All About 202 New Testament: Colossians—Revelation Session 1—Colossians to Philemon

What the Bible Is All About 202 New Testament: Colossians—Revelation Session 8—Hebrews to Revelation

What the Bible Is All About 201 New Testament: Matthew—Philippians Session 2—Matthew

What the Bible Is All About 201 New Testament: Matthew—Philippians Session 5—John

What the Bible Is All About 201 New Testament: Matthew—Philippians Session 8—Romans

What the Bible Is All About 201 New Testament: Matthew—Philippians Session 12—Ephesians

What the Bible Is All About 102 Old Testament: Job—Malachi Session 3—Psalms

Bible Overview with Old Testament Emphasis (13 Sessions):

What the Bible Is All About 101 Old Testament: Genesis—Esther Session 2—Genesis to Joshua

What the Bible Is All About 101 Old Testament: Genesis—Esther Session 8—Judges to Esther

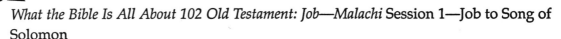

What the Bible Is All About 102 Old Testament: Job—Malachi Session 1—Job to Song of Solomon

What the Bible Is All About 102 Old Testament: Job—Malachi Session 5—Isaiah to Malachi

What the Bible Is All About 201 New Testament: Matthew—Philippians Session 1—The Four Gospels

What the Bible Is All About 201 New Testament: Matthew—Philippians Session 6—Acts to Philippians

What the Bible Is All About 202 New Testament: Colossians—Revelation Session 1—Colossians to Philemon

What the Bible Is All About 202 New Testament: Colossians—Revelation Session 8—Hebrews to Revelation

What the Bible Is All About 101 Old Testament: Genesis—Esther Session 4—Exodus

What the Bible Is All About 101 Old Testament: Genesis—Esther Session 10—1 Samuel

What the Bible Is All About 102 Old Testament: Job—Malachi Session 3—Psalms

What the Bible Is All About 102 Old Testament: Job—Malachi Session 9—Daniel

What the Bible Is All About 102 Old Testament: Job—Malachi Session 11—Obadiah, Jonah and Micah

Bible Overview with New Testament Emphasis (13 Sessions):

What the Bible Is All About 101 Old Testament: Genesis—Esther Session 2—Genesis to Joshua

What the Bible Is All About 101 Old Testament: Genesis—Esther Session 8—Judges to Esther

What the Bible Is All About 102 Old Testament: Job—Malachi Session 1—Job to Song of Solomon

What the Bible Is All About 102 Old Testament: Job—Malachi Session 5—Isaiah to Malachi

What the Bible Is All About 201 New Testament: Matthew—Philippians Session 1—The Four Gospels

What the Bible Is All About 201 New Testament: Matthew—Philippians Session 6—Acts to Philippians

What the Bible Is All About 202 New Testament: Colossians—Revelation Session 1—Colossians to Philemon

What the Bible Is All About 202 New Testament: Colossians—Revelation Session 8—Hebrews to Revelation

What the Bible Is All About 201 New Testament: Matthew—Philippians Session 2—Matthew

What the Bible Is All About 201 New Testament: Matthew—Philippians Session 5—John

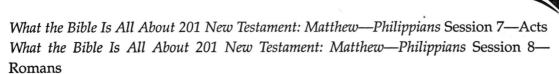

What the Bible Is All About 201 New Testament: Matthew—Philippians Session 7—Acts
What the Bible Is All About 201 New Testament: Matthew—Philippians Session 8—Romans
What the Bible Is All About 202 New Testament: Matthew—Philippians Session 12—Ephesians

FOR 11-SESSION COURSES

What the Bible Is All About 101 Old Testament: Genesis—Esther:

Combine Sessions 5 and 6; combine Sessions 10 and 11.

What the Bible Is All About 102 Old Testament: Job—Malachi:

Combine Sessions 10 and 11; combine Sessions 12 and 13.

What the Bible Is All About 201 New Testament: Matthew—Philippians:

Combine Sessions 9 and 10; combine Sessions 12 and 13.

What the Bible Is All About 202 New Testament: Colossians—Revelation:

Combine Sessions 3 and 4; combine Sessions 5 and 6.

Understanding the Gospels

The purpose of this session is:

- To provide an overview of the Gospels of Matthew, Mark, Luke and John;
- To discover how Jesus Christ is revealed in the Gospels as our Savior and Lord.

In this session, group members will learn:

- Key truths about God's story in the Gospels;
- That Jesus is revealed as our Savior and Lord;
- The basic principle that Jesus Christ came to earth to establish a new covenant with humanity for salvation through His death and resurrection;
- How to apply the truths revealed in the Gospels to their own lives and daily walk with Christ.

KEY VERSES

"An angel of the Lord appeared to him in a dream and said, 'Joseph son of David, do not be afraid to take Mary home as your wife, because what is conceived in her is from the Holy Spirit. She will give birth to a son, and you are to give him the name Jesus, because he will save his people from their sins.'" Matthew 1:20,21

"Jesus went into Galilee, proclaiming the good news of God. 'The time has come,' he said. 'The kingdom of God is near. Repent and believe the good news!'" Mark 1:14,15

"Many have undertaken to draw up an account of the things that have been fulfilled among us, just as they were handed down to us by those who from the first were eyewitnesses and servants of the word. Therefore, since I myself have carefully investigated everything from the beginning, it seemed good also to me to write an orderly account for you, most excellent Theophilus, so that you may know the certainty of the things you have been taught." Luke 1:1-4

"Jesus did many other miraculous signs in the presence of his disciples, which are not recorded in this book. But these are written that you may believe that Jesus is the Christ, the Son of God, and that by believing you may have life in his name." John 20:30,31

BEFORE THE SESSION

- Pray for group members by name, asking the Holy Spirit to teach them the spiritual truths in the Gospel.
- Read chapter 27 in *What the Bible Is All About*.
- Prepare copies of Session 1 handout "God's Story in the Gospels."
- Check off these supplies once you have secured them:
  - _____ A chalkboard and chalk or flip chart or overhead projector with markers.
  - _____ Extra Bibles, pencils and paper for group members.
  - _____ Bring the world, national and local news sections of a Sunday newspaper. Tear the pages so that each group member can have one page of the news.
- If you are having a 90-minute session, carefully read the two option sections right now and pull together any supplies you need for them.
- Read the entire session and look up every passage. Have your Bible *Tuck-In*™ page ready.
- Arrive early and be ready to warmly greet each group member as he or she arrives.
- Memorize the key verses. Share them periodically and ask the group to repeat them as you teach the session.

SECTION ONE: GOD'S STORY (20 MINUTES)

GOD'S STORY IN THE GOSPELS
Objective: To tell God's story so that Christians will apply the truths of the Gospels to their own lives.

Greet everyone as they arrive. Tell the following story, doing the suggested activities as you come to them. Distribute the handout "God's Story in the Gospels" to group members.

This session begins our study of the New Testament or new covenant. In the Old Testament, the Mosaic law defined Israel's relationship with God. Israel was to be a trophy of God's grace and a "light for the Gentiles" (Isaiah 49:6). However, the nation of Israel repeatedly and deliberately rejected the Lord their God. Because of their continued disobedience, God eventually sent His chosen people into captivity in Babylon to teach them to worship Him alone. Eventually some of the Jews returned to Jerusalem, rebuilt the Temple, firmly established the worship of God alone and settled in for a four-hundred-year wait for the promised Messiah.

When Jesus the promised Messiah came to earth, God established a new covenant with humanity through His magnificent grace. This new covenant was made possible only through the death and resurrection of Jesus Christ. According to John 3:16, "God so loved the world [that's us] that he gave his one and only Son [that's Jesus], that whoever believes in him shall not perish but have eternal life [that's an undeserved gift—God's grace]."

Before we do an overview of the Gospels, let's summarize the history of Israel from the time of Malachi (the last book of the Old Testament) to the time of the New Testament:

Draw a line from 333 B.C. to A.D. 30 on the board and write the following names along the line as you recite the brief history of these years:

Alexander the Great	Seleucids rule Israel	Maccabees rule Israel	Rome conquers Israel
333 B.C.	333-152 B.C.	152-137 B.C.	63 B.C.

King Herod is Rome's puppet	Jesus crucified
37—4 B.C.	A.D. 30

1. In 333 B.C., Persia was defeated by Alexander the Great. Alexander and his generals planted Greek cities and culture from Greece to India and Egypt. This spread of Greek culture was called Hellenism.

2. After Alexander's death, one of his generals, Seleucus, began the Seleucid dynasty which oppressed the Jews. One of the Seleucid rulers, Antiochus IV Epiphanes insisted on being worshiped as a god and he profaned the Temple. The Jews revolted.

3. For the brief period of time from 167 to 63 B.C., the Jews had an independent state under the Jewish leaders called the Maccabees who eventually became corrupt.

4. In 63 B.C., the Roman general Pompey conquered Jerusalem and began Roman rule. Herod the Great was appointed governor of Judea and ruled from 37 to 4 B.C. Jesus was born during Herod's reign.

As we begin the New Testament, four words can help us link together the whole of God's Word. Describe the words as you write them down.

Preparation (In the Old Testament, God prepared humanity and history for the coming Messiah.)

Manifestation (In the four Gospels, Christ entered the world, died for humanity and established His Church.)

Appropriation (The Acts and Epistles reveal the ways in which the Lord Jesus was received, appropriated and applied to individual lives.)

Consummation (In the book of Revelation, the outcome of God's perfect plan is revealed.)

These four books about Jesus' life and teachings are called the Gospels. The word "gospel" means "good news." Jesus began His ministry by proclaiming the good news of God (see Mark 1:14,15).

Give everyone a page from the Sunday newspaper. Ask each person to take a pen or pencil and circle every "bad news" headline on their newspaper page and underline each "good news" headline. Have members share how many articles about bad news they find in comparison to the number of articles containing good news. Then invite everyone to read the first chapter of Mark noting all the paragraphs filled with good news and those with bad news. Then discuss:

Would you describe the newspaper as a "gospel?" Why or why not?

In what ways are the Gospels like a newspaper?

How are they unlike newspapers?

The Gospels are unique ancient literature. While they contain biographical and historical facts, they also record the spiritual truths about God's Son—Jesus.

The Gospels were written so that whoever reads them might believe that Jesus is the Son of God and confess Him to be both Lord and Savior (see Luke 1:1-4; John 20:30,31).

Ask for volunteers to answer the question: **What is one fact about Jesus that motivates you to define Him as Lord and/or Savior?** (For example, one might say the resurrection. Another, that Jesus performed mighty miracles. Still another, that

Jesus taught with power and authority, or that Jesus died on the cross for our sins.) Assure group members that they may repeat an answer if someone else has already given that answer.

As group members share, jot down brief summaries of their answers on the board, flip chart or overhead. When everyone has finished, go back over the list and put a check by all the facts that can be found in at least one of the Gospels. This will help group members visualize just how many facts they know about Jesus and how those Gospel-based facts led them to faith in Jesus as their Lord and Savior.

The first three Gospels are called the "synoptic gospels." Synoptic means that they share much of their material in common.

The Gospels of Luke and Matthew seem to follow the order in Mark but at times Luke and Matthew have material in common that is not found in Mark. As three witnesses, each synoptic Gospel writer gives details and background which helps us fill in a more complete picture of Jesus. While the synoptic Gospels of Matthew, Mark and Luke presented their witness in a chronological framework detailing Jesus' life and actions, John focused primarily on the teachings, discourses, signs and miracles of Jesus.

Assign each of three volunteers one of the following passages to read out loud: Matthew 9:9-13; Mark 2:13-17 and Luke 5:27-32. After these have been read, discuss:
What are the similarities between these passages?
What do you think accounts for the similarities?
In what ways are the passages different?
Do the differences diminish or increase the reliability of their witness to the facts? Why?

Each Gospel portrays Jesus from the unique perspective of its author. In Matthew, Jesus is portrayed as King and Messiah with the primary audience being the Jewish people (see Matthew 1:1,17; 2:1-8; 21:1-11; 27:11).

Ask two volunteers to read Matthew 12:22-37; Matthew 20:20-28. Then discuss with the whole group:
How did the Jewish religious leaders respond to Jesus as a king?
What kind of kingdom did Jesus claim to rule over, and what kind of king was He?
How were the citizens of His kingdom to act?

Mark wrote primarily for Romans with a direct, action-packed style. Jesus is portrayed by Mark as the Servant.

There is no geneology of Jesus in Mark because the Romans were not as interested in geneaologies, and they especially would not be interested in the ancestry of a servant (see Mark 10:45).

Have group members volunteer their definitions of a servant. Then ask everyone to read Philippians 2:5-11. Have the whole group help you list all the servant qualities of Jesus.

Luke primarily addressed the Greeks of his day and portrayed Jesus as the perfect Man who is Lord over all creation and people.

The Greek word for Lord, *kurios*, means the head of a household, a master, a person in high position. Luke traced Jesus' geneology from Adam instead of Abraham to demonstrate Jesus' Lordship over all humanity, not just over the Jewish people (see Luke 2:23-37; 4:18-27; 6:5; 7:1-10).

Divide the whole group into three smaller groups. Assign each group one of the following texts: Luke 9:37-62; Luke 10:1-24; Luke 11:1-28. Have each group answer the following questions about the passage:

Over what is Jesus Lord in your passage?

How does He demonstrate His Lordship in each passage?

John proclaimed the Gospel through the signs, miracles, teachings and discourses of Jesus.

He wrote to all who seek a savior so he portrayed Jesus as the Son of God (see John 1:1-5; 8:48-59).

A sign, or miracle, points to Jesus as the Son of God and gives glory (or praise) to God. Read John 2:1-11. Discuss:

What was the purpose of the miracle of turning water into wine? Direct the discussion toward John 2:11.

OPTION ONE: (FOR A 90-MINUTE SESSION)

Four Is Better Than One (15 Minutes)

Make certain that all group members have a blank piece of paper and a pencil or pen. Ask for two men and a woman willing to role-play a parenting situation. Assign the roles of parents and teenager to the three volunteers. Have the following explanation written on a piece of paper or quickly tell them: **You will role-play a situation in which a teenager comes in late at night past curfew and he did not call to say he would be late. He tells his parents that he has just wrecked the family car. He smells of alcohol and he confesses that he has recently gotten a ticket for**

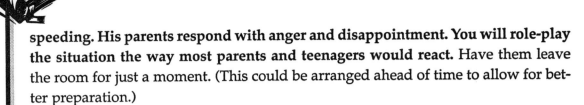

speeding. **His parents respond with anger and disappointment. You will role-play the situation the way most parents and teenagers would react.** Have them leave the room for just a moment. (This could be arranged ahead of time to allow for better preparation.)

Tell the rest of the group to watch the role-play closely. After the performance, ask everyone to write a summary of what they saw. Invite four members to read their summaries. Have the group members note the differences and similarities in the stories. Then discuss:

The Gospels were written by four witnesses to the life and ministry of Jesus. How are four accounts better than just one?

How do you feel about the differences between the accounts?

Does that decrease the reliability of the Gospels or is the total picture enhanced for you? Explain your answer.

Have everyone turn to Matthew 26:57,58; Mark 14:53,54 and Luke 22:54,55. Have volunteers read each account. With the whole group, decide what details each account has that the other two do not. Discuss how these details make the account more complete.

SECTION TWO: GOD'S PERSON (15 MINUTES)

JOHN THE BAPTIST: PREPARING THE WAY

Objective: To discover how John the Baptist prepared people to receive Jesus as Messiah and how John's message prepares us to do the same.

Divide the whole group into four groups and assign one of the following passages to each group:

Group One:	Matthew 3
Group Two:	Mark 1:1-14
Group Three:	Luke 3:1-20
Group Four:	John 1:6-34

Ask the groups to read their verses and summarize the facts about John the Baptist's life and message based on their assigned Gospel. Then with the whole group discuss:

How did John prepare the way for Jesus to come as the Messiah?

What was his message to the people of Jesus' day?

How can that message prepare our hearts to receive Jesus?
In what ways was John like the Old Testament prophets? How was he different?

OPTION TWO: (FOR A 90-MINUTE SESSION)

Keys to the Gospel (15 Minutes)

The introductions and conclusions of the Gospels give us clues as to what that Gospel tells about Jesus' life. Have the group stay in their four small groups. Assign each small group one of the four Gospels, telling them to skim through the first (*except* in Luke read chapter 3) and last chapters (*except* in John read chapter 20). Write the following questions on the board, flip chart or overhead and list the titles for Jesus. Each group is to select the title that they believe best represents how their assigned Gospel portrays Jesus (from those listed below).

> **How does your assigned Gospel portray Jesus?**
>
> **Which verse or verses would support this Gospel's title for Jesus?**

Possible answers: The Gospel of Matthew has a geneology of David's line which supports Jesus' kingship and concludes with the King issuing marching orders to His disciples. The Gospel of Mark has no geneology because a servant doesn't need one, and it portrays Jesus as a laborer with His disciples in Mark 16:20. The Gospel of Luke recites the geneology of Jesus back through Adam (see Luke 3:23-38) and it concludes with Jesus the Lord ascending into heaven. In the first chapter of John, Jesus is portrayed both as the Word of God and as divine and John closed his Gospel with the claim that all the books in the world could not contain all Jesus had done.

Put these two lists on the board and ask the group to match the titles of Jesus with the Gospel that uses that title as its theme (they are not in the correct order):

Matthew	Son of God
Mark	Perfect Man and Lord
Luke	Messiah and King
John	Servant

Session
1

SECTION THREE: GOD'S SON (15 MINUTES)

JESUS CHRIST REVEALED IN THE GOSPELS AS SAVIOR AND LORD
Objective: To see how Jesus is revealed in the Gospels as our Savior and Lord.

Remaining in the same four groups, assign each group one of the Gospels. On their handouts in the section entitled "Pictures of Jesus in the Gospels" is a statement and a passage about Jesus from each Gospel. Have each group read their assigned Gospel passage. Then ask each group to discuss in what ways their text supports the statement. Instruct each group to summarize in one sentence how the passage illustrates the statement. Invite each group to share their summary statement with the other groups.

PURSUING GOD (5 MINUTES)

NEXT STEPS I NEED TO TAKE
Objective: To take a realistic assessment of one's relationship with Jesus and how that relationship might grow closer in the coming week.

In the same four groups, ask each person to share which of the four "pictures" of Jesus from the Section Three activity means the most to them and why. Also have them share one step they need to take to grow closer to the Savior each day.

PRAYER (5 MINUTES)

Objective: To pray as a group thanking God for His good news in Jesus Christ.

Have the whole group form a circle. Have a short time of praise for anyone who wishes to share one name or title for Jesus that they are most thankful for, such as Savior, Lord, Master, Servant, Friend, etc.

As the leader, close the sharing time with a prayer of thanksgiving that Jesus is our Lord and Savior.

Session 1 Bible *Tuck-In*™

UNDERSTANDING THE GOSPELS

The purpose of this session is:

- To provide an overview of the Gospels of Matthew, Mark, Luke and John.
- To discover how Jesus Christ is revealed in the Gospels as Lord and Savior.

KEY VERSES

"An angel of the Lord appeared to him in a dream and said, 'Joseph son of David, do not be afraid to take Mary home as your wife, because what is conceived in her is from the Holy Spirit. She will give birth to a son, and you are to give him the name Jesus, because he will save his people from their sins.'" Matthew 1:20,21

"Jesus went into Galilee, proclaiming the good news of God. 'The time has come,' he said. 'The kingdom of God is near. Repent and believe the good news!'" Mark 1:14,15

"Many have undertaken to draw up an account of the things that have been fulfilled among us, just as they were handed down to us by those who from the first were eyewitnesses and servants of the word. Therefore, since I myself have carefully investigated everything from the beginning, it seemed good also to me to write an orderly account for you,

---

How does your Gospel portray Jesus?
Which verse or verses would support this Gospel's title for Jesus?

- Have the group match the titles with the Gospels.

SECTION THREE: GOD'S SON (15 MINUTES)

JESUS CHRIST REVEALED IN THE GOSPELS AS SAVIOR AND LORD

- Remaining in the same four groups, assign each group one of the Gospels. On their handouts in the section entitled "Pictures of Jesus in the Gospels," have each group read their assigned Gospel passage. Then ask each group to discuss in what ways their text supports their statement.

Instruct each group to summarize in one sentence how the passage illustrates the statement.

- Invite each group to share their summary statement.

PURSUING GOD (5 MINUTES)

NEXT STEPS I NEED TO TAKE

- In the same four small groups, ask each person to share which of the four "pictures" of Jesus means the most to them and why. Also have them share one step they need to take to grow closer to the Savior each day.

PRAYER (5 MINUTES)

- Have the whole group form a circle. Have a short time of praise for anyone who wishes to share one name or title for Jesus that they are most thankful for.
- As the leader, close the sharing time with a prayer of thanksgiving that Jesus is our Lord and Savior.

most excellent Theophilus, so that you may know the certainty of the things you have been taught." Luke 1:1-4

"Jesus did many other miraculous signs in the presence of his disciples, which are not recorded in this book. But these are written that you may believe that Jesus is the Christ, the Son of God, and that by believing you may have life in his name." John 20:30,31

SECTION ONE: GOD'S STORY (20 MINUTES)

GOD'S STORY IN THE GOSPELS

- Greet everyone as they arrive. Tell the story of the Gospels, doing the suggested activities as you come to them. Distribute the handout "God's Story in the Gospels" to group members.

OPTION ONE: (FOR A 90-MINUTE SESSION)

Four Is Better Than One (15 Minutes)

- Ask for two men and a woman willing to role-play a parenting situation. Explain the role-play to them.
- Tell the rest of the group to watch the role-play closely. After the performance, ask everyone to write a summary of what they saw. Invite four members to read their summaries. Note the differences and similarities between the stories. Then discuss:

The Gospels were written by four witnesses to the life and ministry of Jesus. How are four accounts better than just one? How do you feel about the differences between the accounts? Does that decrease the reliability of the Gospels or is the total picture enhanced for you? Explain your answer.

- Fold -

- Have everyone turn to Matthew 26:57,58; Mark 14:53,54 and Luke 22:54,55. With the whole group, decide what details each account has that the other two do not. Discuss how these details make the account more complete.

SECTION TWO: GOD'S PERSON (15 MINUTES)

JOHN THE BAPTIST: PREPARING THE WAY

- Divide the whole group into four groups and assign one of the following passages to each group: Matthew 3; Mark 1:1-14; Luke 3:1-20; John 1:6-34
- Ask each group to read through their verses and summarize John's life and message based on their assigned passage. Discuss:

How did John prepare the way for Jesus to come as the Messiah to Israel?

What was his message to the people of Jesus' day?

How does that message prepare our hearts to receive Jesus?

In what ways was John like the Old Testament prophets?

How was he different?

OPTION TWO: (FOR A 90-MINUTE SESSION)

Keys to the Gospel (15 Minutes)

- Have the group stay in their four small groups. Assign each small group one of the four Gospels, telling them to scan the first (except in Luke read chapter 3) and last chapters (except in John read chapter 20). Write the following questions on the board, flip chart or overhead and list the titles for Jesus. Each group is to select the title that they believe best represents how their assigned Gospel portrays Jesus (from those listed).

GOD'S STORY IN THE GOSPELS

Notes about the period of time between the Old and New Testaments:

As we begin the New Testament, four words can help us link together the whole of God's Word:

Preparation: _____

Manifestation: _____

Appropriation: _____

Consummation: _____

1. These four books about Jesus' life and teachings are called the Gospels. The word "gospel" means "good news." Jesus began His ministry proclaiming the good news of God (see Mark 1:14,15).

   Notes:

2. The Gospels are unique ancient literature. While they contain biographical and historical facts, they also record the spiritual truths about God's son—Jesus.

   Notes:

3. The first three Gospels are called the "synoptic gospels." Synoptic means that they share much of their material in common.

   Notes:

CONTINUED

4. Each Gospel portrays Jesus from the unique perspective of its author. In Matthew, Jesus is portrayed as King and Messiah with the primary audience being the Jewish people (see Matthew 1:1,17; 2:1-8; 21:1-11; 27:11).

Notes:

5. Mark wrote primarily for Romans with a direct, action-packed style. Jesus is portrayed by Mark as the Servant.

Notes:

6. Luke primarily addressed the Greeks of his day and portrayed Jesus as the perfect Man who is Lord over all creation and people.

Notes:

7. John proclaimed the Gospel through the signs, miracles, teachings and discourses of Jesus.

Notes:

CONTINUED

PICTURES OF JESUS IN THE GOSPELS

- Matthew emphasized the coming of a *Promised* Messiah (Matthew 1:18-23).

- Mark emphasized the life of a *Powerful* Messiah (Mark 6:45-56).

- Luke emphasized the grace of a *Perfect Savior* (Luke 4:1-22)

- John emphasized the possession of a *Personal Savior* (John 14:9-17)

Summarize in one sentence how the passage illustrates the statement about your assigned Gospel:

CONTINUED

Before the next session, read:

Sunday: The King Born (Matthew 1:18—2:23)

Monday: The King Begins Work (Matthew 4:1-25)

Tuesday: The King States Kingdom Laws (Matthew 5:1-17,41-48; 6:19-34)

Wednesday: The King and His Followers (Matthew 10:1-33)

Thursday: The Kingdom Mysteries (Matthew 13:1-52)

Friday: The King Offers Himself As King (Matthew 21:1-11)

Saturday: The King Will Return (Matthew 25:14-16)

Understanding Matthew

The purpose of this session is:

- To provide an overview of the Gospel of Matthew;
- To discover how Jesus Christ is revealed in Matthew as the promised Messiah.

In this session, group members will learn:

- Key truths about God's story in Matthew;
- That Jesus is revealed as the promised Messiah;
- The basic principle that Jesus fulfilled all of the Old Testament prophecies concerning His coming and that He proclaimed the requirements of living in God's Kingdom;
- How to apply the truths revealed in Matthew to our daily walk with Jesus Christ.

KEY VERSES

"Do not think that I have come to abolish the Law or the Prophets; I have not come to abolish them but to fulfill them." Matthew 5:17

"'But what about you?' [Jesus] asked. 'Who do you say I am?'

"Simon Peter answered, 'You are the Christ, the Son of the living God.' Jesus replied, 'Blessed are you, Simon son of Jonah, for this was not revealed to you by man, but by my Father in heaven.'" Matthew 16:15-17

"Jesus stood before the governor [Pilate], and the governor asked him, 'Are you the king of the Jews?'

'Yes, it is as you say,' Jesus replied." Matthew 27:11

"Then Jesus came to them and said, 'All authority in heaven and on earth has been given to me. Therefore go and make disciples of all nations, baptizing them in the name of the Father and of the Son and of the Holy Spirit, and teaching them to obey everything I have commanded you. And surely I am with you always, to the very end of the age.'" Matthew 28:18,19

BEFORE THE SESSION

- Pray for group members by name, asking the Holy Spirit to reveal to them the spiritual truths in Matthew.
- Read Chapter 28 in *What the Bible Is All About*

- Prepare copies of the Session 2 handout "God's Story in Matthew."
- Check off these supplies once you have secured them:
  _____ A chalkboard and chalk or flip chart or overhead projector with markers.
  _____ Extra Bibles, pencils and paper for group members.
  _____ Four pieces of poster board and four sets of colored felt-tip pens if you are doing Option One.
- If you are having a 90-minute session, carefully read the two option sections right now and pull together any supplies you need for them.
- Read the entire session and look up every passage. Have your Bible *Tuck-In*™ page ready.
- Arrive early and be ready to warmly greet each group member as he or she arrives.
- Memorize the key verses. Share them periodically and ask the group to repeat them as you teach the session.

SECTION ONE: GOD'S STORY (20 MINUTES)

GOD'S STORY IN MATTHEW

Objective: To tell God's story so that Christians will apply the truths in Matthew to their own lives.

Greet everyone as they arrive. Tell the following story, doing the suggested activities as you come to them. Distribute the handout "God's Story in Matthew" to group members.

The Promised King and Messiah

Matthew's main objective in his Gospel was to show that Jesus is the long-await-ed Messiah, the promised Son of David, who fulfilled the Old Testament prophe-cies. His Gospel begins: "A record of the genealogy of Jesus Christ [the Messiah] the son of David [king], the son of Abraham [a Jew]" (Matthew 1:1). As the son of David, Jesus is the promised King who has established the Davidic throne forev-er (see 2 Samuel 7:13,16). As the son of Abraham, Jesus is the promised Seed of Abraham who will bless all of the peoples on the earth (see Genesis 12:3; 22:18) and be the sacrifice that God provides (see Genesis 22:13-18) for the sins of the world. Jesus is born during the reign of Herod the Great, a puppet king for Rome in Jerusalem (see Matthew 2).

Read Galatians 4:4 and Romans 5:6. Discuss: **What are some factors that made this era the right time in history for Jesus' first coming ?** After a short discussion, summarize the following factors that most scholars believe to be important, historical conditions that made it the "right time" for Jesus to come.

- **Oppressed by Roman rule, the Jewish people were looking for the promised Messiah. Herod the Great and Herod Antipas were hated by the Jews who longed for the Messiah's deliverance.**
- **Roman and Greek religions were empty and they were losing their appeal throughout the Roman Empire.**
- *Pax Romana*—**Roman peace—made the known world at that time a relatively safe place and accessible for extensive travel and commerce.**
- **The common languages of the day—Greek and Latin—made it possible to communicate throughout the Roman Empire.**

The King's Life

Matthew revealed the royal lineage of Jesus, the promised King and Messiah, from the house of David. Matthew traced Jesus' life as the anointed Messiah— King of Israel—beginning with the King's name (see Matthew 1:23) **and culminating with the King's victory over our greatest enemy—death** (see 28:6).

Have each person refer to the section titled "Jesus as King in Matthew" on their handouts. Form pairs. Have the pairs work together to discover the progression of Jesus revealed as the King in Matthew. Then ask them to share with their partners what new thing they have just learned that either surprised them or touched their hearts.

The King's Message

In Matthew, King Jesus proclaimed that to enter the kingdom of God, people must repent (see Matthew 4:17) **and follow Him** (see Matthew 4:19; 8:22; 10:37,38; 16:24; 19:21).

Invite two or three volunteers to share the time in their lives when they clearly heard Jesus call them to follow Him, how they obeyed that call, and what occurred as a result of their obedience.

The King's Law

The Jewish people held Moses in highest esteem as Israel's lawgiver. Matthew portrayed Jesus as the ultimate Lawgiver with even more authority than Moses. As King and Lawgiver, Jesus proclaimed the essential meaning of Mosaic law in the Sermon on the Mount (see Matthew 5—7). **Jesus unequivocally stated that He came to fulfill the Mosaic law, not abolish it** (see Matthew 5:17-20) **and that life in God's kingdom is filled with blessing** (see Matthew 5:3-12).

Divide the class into three groups. Assign one chapter of the Sermon on the Mount in Matthew 5; 6; 7 to each group. Tell them to use the section on their handouts entitled "The Principles of Kingdom Living" and identify the basic law or principle for their assigned passage. The passages within each chapter could be divided up between the group members.

The King Rejected

Though Jesus was the promised Messiah and King, some Jewish people believed Him, yet many others rejected Him. Jesus taught that the Kingdom of God would be taken from the Jewish nation as a whole and given to anyone willing to receive Him as King and Savior (see Matthew 21:33-43). Those who confess Him as the Messiah—the Christ—will form the Church (*ecclesia* which means "called out ones"), a new people made up of both Jews and Gentiles who are called out of the kingdom of this world and into God's kingdom (see Matthew 16:18,19).

Read Matthew 16:13-19 in unison. Ask any group members who may wish to do so to share what being a part of the Church of Jesus Christ means to them.

The King Crucified

Some of the people acknowledged Jesus as King when He triumphantly rode into Jerusalem on the Sunday before Passover (see Matthew 21:1-9). However, by Friday Jesus was betrayed to the Jewish leaders by Judas, and His other disciples had deserted Him. In a sham of a Jewish trial, Jesus was convicted of blasphemy, then sent to Pilate. Giving into Jesus' enemies, Pilate sentenced the innocent Jesus to death by crucifixion with common criminals. Jesus suffered this excruciating death on the cross for *our* sins (see Matthew 26—27).

Invite any class members who are willing to share their completion to one of the following statements:
The most meaningful thing to me about the crucifixion is ....
The most meaningful thing to me about the Last Supper is ....

The King Triumphant

Imagine the intense grief of Jesus' followers as they awoke that first Sunday after His death and burial. What joy they experienced as they finally realized that He had been raised from death as He had promised. There are some who would try to discredit the fact of Jesus' death and resurrection. Read Matthew 27:45—28:20 yourself looking for evidences that Jesus' resurrection really did occur.

Have the group members call out the evidences that they find in these verses that give proof of the Resurrection as you list the findings on the board, flip chart or overhead. Discuss:
What does the resurrection of Jesus mean to us as believers?
How should the fact of the Resurrection affect our fulfillment of the Great Commission (see Matthew 28:18-20)?

OPTION ONE: (FOR A 90-MINUTE SESSION)

Life's Most Important Question (15 Minutes)

Ask: **What are the different responses the unbelieving and uninformed world have to the question posed by Jesus in Matthew 16:13: "'Who do people say the Son of Man is?'"** List their reponses on the board, flip chart or overhead. Then have them suggest responses that Christians should have to life's most important question: Who do you say that He is?

Divide the group into four small groups. Give each small group a piece of poster board and some colored felt-tip pens. Assign each group one of the following titles of Jesus as proclaimed by Matthew. Give them about five minutes to draw a poster illustrating their assigned title.

Group One:	Christ or Messiah (Matthew 1:16)
Group Two:	Son of the Living God (Matthew 16:16)
Group Three:	King (Matthew 2:2)
Group Four:	Son of David (Matthew 1:1)

After about five minutes, ask each small group to explain their poster to the whole group, and then with the whole group discuss:

How would you explain the meaning of these titles to an unbeliever?

Which title means the most to you and why?

SECTION TWO: GOD'S PERSON (15 MINUTES)

JESUS: THE PROMISED KING AND MESSIAH

Objective: To discover Jesus the King as the fulfillment of Old Testament prophecies in Matthew.

Have each of the following Scripture references written on a separate slip of paper. Hand out each of the slips of paper to group members. If there are more

verses than group members, give members two or more verses to read. Give them a minute or two to find and familiarize themselves with their assigned verse(s). Have the first person read the first Matthew passage and then the one who has the corresponding Old Testament verse stands up and reads his or her verse and reference. Group members may record the corresponding verses on the handout entitled "New Testament Fulfillment of Old Testament Prophesies."

Matthew 1:22,23	(Isaiah 7:14; 8:8,10)
Matthew 2:5,6	(Micah 5:2)
Matthew 2:15,16	(Hosea 11:1)
Matthew 2:17,18	(Jeremiah 31:15)
Matthew 3:3	(Isaiah 40:3; Malachi 3:1)
Matthew 4:14-16	(Isaiah 9:1,2)
Matthew 8:17	(Isaiah 53:4)
Matthew 12:17-21	(Isaiah 42:1-4)
Matthew 12:39-41	(Jonah 1:2,17)
Matthew 13:35	(Psalm 78:2)
Matthew 21:4,5	(Zechariah 9:9)
Matthew 27:9,10	(Zechariah 11:12,13; Jeremiah 32:6-9)

OPTION TWO: (FOR A 90-MINUTE SESSION)

Jesus' Last Week—The Passion Narrative (15 Minutes)

On the handout 2 section titled "Jesus' Last Week" the events of Jesus' last week—the Passion Week—are listed out of order. Give each group member a copy or display a copy using an overhead projector. With the whole group, try to number the events in the correct sequence as they appear in Matthew without looking at the Bible. Then correct the group's order from the list below if necessary.

1. Triumphal Entry
2. Cleansing the Temple
3. The Lord's Supper
4. Judas's Betrayal
5. Trial Before the Jewish Court—the Sanhedrin
6. Peter's Denial of Jesus
7. Trial Before Pilate
8. The Crucifixion
9. The Resurrection

SECTION THREE: GOD'S SON (15 MINUTES)

JESUS CHRIST REVEALED AS THE PROMISED KING

Objective: To see how Jesus is revealed in Matthew as the promised King.

A central theme to Jesus' teaching is the Kingdom of Heaven—also called the Kingdom of God. Jesus often used parables. A parable is a story from everyday life that teaches an essential truth about God. From the parables we learn how we are to live in His Kingdom.

Using the same four groups from Option One (or form four groups if you didn't do Option One), assign one of the following parables to each group. Instruct them that in five minutes they will make a presentation of their parable to the whole group. They may act it out, mime, create a paraphrase or simply summarize the parable for the group. Write the following questions on the board, flip chart or overhead and ask the groups to be able to share their answers concerning their assigned parable:

What does this parable teach about Jesus?

What does this parable teach about how we are to live in the Kingdom?

Group One:	The Weeds—Matthew 13:24-30,36-43
Group Two:	The Ten Virgins—Matthew 25:1-13
Group Three:	The Sheep and Goats—Matthew 25:31-46
Group Four:	The Vineyard—Matthew 20:1-16

After all the groups have shared their parables and the truths, discuss: **When Jesus is King and Lord over our lives, what should our response to Him be?**

PURSUING GOD (5 MINUTES)

NEXT STEPS I NEED TO TAKE

Objective: To take a realistic assessment of one's relationship with Jesus and how that relationship might grow closer in the coming week.

Ask each person to read through the Beatitudes in Matthew 5:1-12. Invite them to find a partner and share the "be-attitude" that is most often expressed in his or her life and the one that needs the most cultivation. Ask the pairs to tell one another the next step they will take to allow the Holy Spirit to grow that attitude in their lives. List the Beatitude qualities on the board while they are sharing so that it will be easier for them to refer to the list:

Poor in Spirit
Mourn for sin
Meek/humble/gentle
Hunger and thirst for righteousness
Merciful
Pure in heart
Peacemaker
Joy in persecution

PRAYER (5 MINUTES)

Objective: To pray through the Great Commission.

Read Matthew 28:18-20 to the whole group. Ask the group members to pray out loud the following prayer echoing one phrase at a time after you:

**King Jesus, in obedience to You,
I will go and seek to make disciples of all those in the world around me,
Inviting them to be baptized in the name of the Father, Son and Holy Spirit,
Teaching them to obey everything You have commanded.
Thank You for the power and authority You have given me to do this, in Your Name. Amen.**

Session 2 Bible *Tuck-In*™

UNDERSTANDING MATTHEW

The purpose of this session is:

- To provide an overview of the Gospel of Matthew;
- To discover how Jesus Christ is revealed in Matthew as the promised Messiah.

KEY VERSES

"Do not think that I have come to abolish the Law or the Prophets; I have not come to abolish them but to fulfill them." Matthew 5:17

"'But what about you?'' [Jesus] asked. 'Who do you say I am?' Simon Peter answered, 'You are the Christ, the Son of the living God.' Jesus replied, 'Blessed are you, Simon son of Jonah, for this was not revealed to you by man, but by my Father in heaven.''' Matthew 16:15-17

"Jesus stood before the governor [Pilate], and the governor asked him, 'Are you the king of the Jews?' 'Yes, it is as you say,' Jesus replied." Matthew 27:11

"Then Jesus came to them and said, 'All authority in heaven and on earth has been given to me. Therefore go and make disciples of all nations, baptizing them in the name of the Father and of the Son and of the Holy Spirit, and teaching them to

---

create a paraphrase or simply summarize the parable for the group. Write the following questions on the board, flip chart or overhead and ask the groups to be able to share their answers concerning their assigned parable:

What does this parable teach about Jesus?

What does this parable teach about how we are to live in the Kingdom?

- After all the groups have shared, discuss: **When Jesus is King and Lord over our lives, what should our response to Him be?**

PURSUING GOD (5 MINUTES)

NEXT STEPS I NEED TO TAKE

- Ask each person to read Matthew 5:1-12. Invite the pairs to share the "be-attitude" that is most often expressed in their lives and the one that needs the most cultivation. Ask them to tell one another the next step they will take to allow the Holy Spirit to grow that attitude in their lives. List the qualities on the board while they are sharing so that it will be easier for them to refer to the list.

PRAYER (5 MINUTES)

- Read Matthew 28:18-20 to the whole group. Ask the group members to pray out loud the following prayer echoing one phrase at a time after you:

King Jesus, in obedience to You, I will go and seek to make disciples of all those in the world around me, inviting them to be baptized in the name of the Father, Son and Holy Spirit, teaching them to obey everything You have commanded. Thank You for the power and authority You have given me to do this, in Your Name. Amen.

obey everything I have commanded you. And surely I am with you always, to the very end of the age.'" Matthew 28:18,19

SECTION ONE: GOD'S STORY (20 MINUTES)

GOD'S STORY IN MATTHEW

• Greet everyone as they arrive. Tell the story in Matthew, doing the suggested activities as you come to them. Distribute the handout "God's Story in Matthew" to group members.

OPTION ONE: (FOR A 90-MINUTE SESSION)

Life's Most Important Question (15 Minutes)

• Ask: What are the different responses the unbelieving and uninformed world have to the question posed by Jesus in Matthew 16:13: "Who do people say the Son of Man is?" List their responses. Then have them suggest responses that Christians have to life's most important question: **Who do you say that He is?**

• Divide the group into four groups. Give each group a piece of poster board and felt-tip pens. Assign each group one of the following titles of Jesus. Have them draw a poster illustrating their assigned title. Group One: Christ or Messiah; Group Two: Son of the Living God; Group Three: King; Group Four: Son of David.

• After five minutes, share posters, and then discuss: **How would you explain the meaning of these titles to an unbeliever? Which title means the most to you and why?**

------- Fold -------

SECTION TWO: GOD'S PERSON (15 MINUTES)

JESUS: THE PROMISED KING AND MESSIAH

• Hand out each of the Scripture reference papers to group members. Give them a minute or two to find and familiarize themselves with their assigned verse(s). Have the first person read the first Matthew passage and then the one who has the corresponding Old Testament verse stands up and reads his or her verse and reference. Group members may record the corresponding verses on the handout entitled "New Testament Fulfillment of Old Testament Prophesies."

OPTION TWO: (FOR A 90-MINUTE SESSION)

Jesus' Last Week—The Passion Narrative (15 Minutes)

• On the handout section titled "Jesus' Last Week" the events of Jesus' last week—the Passion Week—are listed out of order. With the whole group, try to number the events in the correct sequence as they appear in Matthew without looking at the Bible. Then correct the group's order if necessary.

SECTION THREE: GOD'S SON (15 MINUTES)

JESUS CHRIST REVEALED AS THE PROMISED KING

• Using the same four groups from Option One (or form four groups if you didn't do Option One), assign one of the following parables to each group: Group One: Matthew 13:24-30,36-43; Group Two: Matthew 25:1-13; Group Three: Matthew 25:31-46; Group Four: Matthew 20:1-16.

• Instruct them that in five minutes they will act out, mime,

GOD'S STORY IN MATTHEW

1. The Promised King and Messiah

   Notes:

2. The King's Life

   Notes:

Jesus as King in Matthew

Briefly jot down how the following passages describe Jesus as the King.

   a. A king's name (1:23) _____

   b. A king's position (2:6) _____

   c. A king's announcement (3:3) _____

   d. A king's coronation (3:17) _____

   e. A king's due respect (4:10) _____

   f. A king's proclamation (5:2) _____

   g. A king's loyalty (12:30) _____

   h. A king's enemies (16:21; 2:13-18) _____

   i. A king's love (20:28) _____

   j. A king's glory (25:31,34) _____

   k. A king's sacrifice (27:35,37) _____

   l. A king's victory (28:6) _____

3. The King's Message

   Notes:

4. The King's Law

   Notes:

5. The King Rejected

   Notes:

6. The King Crucified

   Notes:

7. The King Triumphant

   Notes:

THE PRINCIPLES OF KINGDOM LIVING (MATTHEW 5—7)
Chapter 5

    1. The Beatitudes (5:1-11) _____

    2. Salt and Light (5:13-16) _____

    3. The Law (5:17-20) _____

    4. Murder (5:21-26) _____

    5. Adultery (5:27-30) _____

    6. Divorce (5:31-32) _____

CONTINUED

7. Oaths (5:33-37) _____
8. An eye for an eye (5:38-42) _____
9. Enemies (5:43-48) _____

Chapter 6
10. Giving (6:1-4) _____
11. Praying (6:5-15) _____
12. Fasting (6:16-18) _____
13. Treasures (6:19-24) _____

Chapter 7
14. Judging Others (7:1-6) _____
15. Asking (7:7-12) _____
16. Entering (7:13-14) _____
17. Bearing Fruit (7:15-23) _____
18. Building on His Words (7:24-27) _____

Before the next session, read:
Sunday: The Servant's Coming and Testing (Mark 1:1-20)
Monday: The Servant Working (Mark 2:1—3:25)
Tuesday: The Servant Speaking (Mark 4:1—6:13)
Wednesday: The Servant's Miracles (Mark 6:32—8:26)
Thursday: The Servant's Revelation (Mark 8:27—10:34)
Friday: The Servant's Rejection (Mark 11:1—12:44)
Saturday: The Servant's Death and Triumph (Mark 14:1—16:20)

SESSION 2

NEW TESTAMENT FULFILLMENT OF OLD TESTAMENT PROPHESIES

Matthew 1:22,23 _____

Matthew 2:5,6 _____

Matthew 2:15,16 _____

Matthew 2:17,18 _____

Matthew 3:3 _____

Matthew 4:14-16 _____

Matthew 8:17 _____

Matthew 12:17-21 _____

Matthew 12:39-41 _____

Matthew 13:35 _____

Matthew 21:4,5 _____

Matthew 27:9,10 _____

JESUS' LAST WEEK

Number in the correct sequence from 1 to 9 the following events in Jesus' last week:

____ The Resurrection

____ Trial Before the Jewish Court—the Sanhedrin

____ The Crucifixion

____ Trial Before Pilate

____ Peter's Denial of Jesus

____ The Lord's Supper

____ Judas's Betrayal

____ The Triumphal Entry

____ Cleansing the Temple

Understanding Mark

The purpose of this session is:

- To provide an overview of the Gospel of Mark;
- To discover how Jesus Christ is revealed in Mark as the Servant of God.

In this session, group members will learn:

- Key truths about God's story in Mark;
- That Jesus is revealed as the Servant of God;
- The basic principle that just as Jesus was God's Servant, we are to be His servants completing His work on earth;
- How to apply the truths revealed in Mark to their daily lives.

KEY VERSES

"'For even the Son of Man did not come to be served, but to serve, and to give his life as a ransom for many.'" Mark 10:45

"Jesus went into Galilee, proclaiming the good news of God. 'The time has come,' he said. 'The kingdom of God is near. Repent and believe the good news!'" Mark 1:14,15

"'For whoever wants to save his life will lose it, but whoever loses his life for me and for the gospel will save it.'" Mark 8:35

BEFORE THE SESSION

- Pray for group members by name, asking the Holy Spirit to reveal to them the spiritual truths in Mark.
- Read chapter 29 in *What the Bible Is All About*.
- Prepare copies of the Session 3 handout "God's Story in Mark" for all group members.
- Check off the following supplies once you have secured them:
  ____ A chalkboard and chalk or flip chart or overhead projector with markers.
  ____ Extra Bibles, pencils and paper for group members.
- If you are having a 90-minute session, carefully read the two option sections right now and pull together any additional supplies you need for them.

- Read the entire session and look up every passage. Have your Bible *Tuck-In*™ page ready.
- Arrive early and be ready to warmly greet each group member as he or she arrives.
- Memorize the key verses. Share them periodically and ask the group to repeat them as you teach the session.

SECTION ONE: GOD'S STORY (20 MINUTES)

GOD'S STORY IN MARK

Objective: To tell God's story so that Christians will apply the truths of the Gospel of Mark to their own lives.

Greet everyone as they arrive. Tell the following story, doing the suggested activities as you come to them. Distribute the handout "God's Story in Mark" to group members.

Mark is the shortest Gospel. It contains 16 chapters and only 4 parables and it portrays Jesus as the perfect Servant of God.

Using none of the divine titles for Jesus that we find in the other Gospels, Mark referred to Jesus as the "Teacher" or "Rabbi" whose purpose was to serve God and humanity.

Read Mark 9:33-35 and 10:42-45. Discuss:

How did Jesus best demonstrate this principle of being a servant?

What are some practical ways in which believers can apply this teaching?

The Servant Prepared (Mark 1:1-13)

Mark's Gospel begins with the preparation of Jesus' ministry before He began to call His disciples and proclaim the gospel message (see Mark 1:14-20).

Ask the group members to read Mark 1:1-13 and to find five different ways that God prepared Jesus for ministry. List their findings on the board. That list should include: Jesus was prepared by (1) John the Baptist's work (vv. 1-8); (2) baptism (v. 9); (3) receiving the Holy Spirit (v. 10); (4) divine call (v. 11); and (5) testing (vv. 12,13).

The Servant Working (Mark 1:14—8:30)

The ministry and work of Jesus continued without a break in Mark. Jesus taught his followers and performed miracles with power and authority throughout Mark's Gospel (see Mark 1:21-28).

Have everyone refer to their handouts under this section. Working in groups of four, ask the group members to divide the verses between them, complete their handouts and share their answers with one another. Have the whole group share the various ways that Jesus demonstrated His authority and power.

The Servant Rejected (Mark 8:31—15:47)

Jesus was rejected by the Jewish rulers and the masses, deserted by His own disciples (see Mark 8:31,14:10,11,27-31,43-46,66-71) **tried, beaten, crucified and buried.**

As a group discuss:

What are some of the reasons the Jewish people rejected Jesus?

Why do people reject Jesus today?

The Servant Exalted (Mark 16:1-20)

God exalted His Servant, Jesus, by raising Him from the dead and seating Him on His right hand (see Mark 16:19,20).

Read 1 Corinthians 15:58. **The Servant of God as the risen Lord is still working in our midst as He works in and through us. Where do you see God at work today in and through your life, the Church and the world?**

OPTION ONE: (FOR A 90-MINUTE SESSION)

Parables about the Seeds (15 Minutes)

Ask everyone to follow along in their Bibles as you read Mark 4:1-20 out loud. Then discuss:

Why won't seeds grow on hard ground?

What would make it possible for the seeds to grow?

How can we best prepare our hearts for receiving the seed of God's Word?

Where do we need to be sowing God's seed?

Now read Mark 4:26-29 to the group. Show the group an apple. Ask group members to guess how many seeds are in the apple and write down their estimates on the back of their handouts. Cut open the apple, count the seeds and see who came closest to guessing the correct amount. Then ask, **How many apples are in a seed? Of course, no one knows that answer but God.** Discuss the parable in light of how God brings a harvest far beyond our efforts.

Finally, read Mark 4:30-32. Give each group member a mustard seed (or similar small seed). Have them silently consider how this small seed can grow into such a large plant. Ask for volunteers to share about a time when a small seed of faith in God produced a great blessing or harvest in their lives.

Section Two: God's Person (15 Minutes)

Jesus: The Servant At Prayer

Objective: To discover Jesus, the Servant, at prayer.

Read Mark 1:35 and 14:32-40. Say: **Jesus received the strength to serve and to face the cross through prayer. We will discover more about praying for that kind of strength for our own lives.**

Across the top of the board, flip chart or overhead, write the following titles:

Hindrances to Prayer   **Aids to Prayer**   **Kinds of Prayers**

Ask the group to help you list appropriate answers under each topic. Invite two or three to share testimonies of times when they prayed and God gave them strength to face a difficult time in life.

Read Mark 9:17-29 to the group, then discuss:

What kinds of situations require intense prayer and fasting?

Why do we often neglect praying before we move ahead in tough situations?

What can we learn from Jesus praying before He faced the cross?

OPTION TWO: (FOR A 90-MINUTE SESSION)

The Servant of God in Power and Authority

Divide the whole group into three groups. Assign each group one chapter from Mark 6—8. Say: **Each of these chapters contains more than one incident where Jesus, God's Servant, demonstrated His power and authority. In your small group, decide on one incident from your assigned chapter. Prepare a frozen-motion sculpture or picture using everyone in your group. You may leave the room if necessary to practice your sculptures or frozen pictures.**

After five to seven minutes, have each group present their picture and have the rest of the groups try to guess the story. After all three stories have been portrayed, discuss with the whole group:

In what ways did these stories portray the authority and power of Jesus?

Why did those around Jesus have such a difficult time understanding who He was?

Would we have reacted any differently? Why or why not?

SECTION THREE: GOD'S SON (15 MINUTES)

JESUS CHRIST REVEALED AS THE SERVANT WHO FORGIVES

Objective: To see how Jesus is revealed in Mark as the Servant who forgives sin.

Have everyone read Mark 2:1-12. Say: **In the Greek, the word *sozo* means both to save and to heal. In this story, Jesus heals the man of both his sin and his physical affliction. Only God's Messiah has the authority to forgive sin and the power to heal the sick.**

Give each group member a pencil or pen and a piece of paper. Ask everyone to turn to Mark 7:20-23. Explain that this is a list of sins that Jesus gave. Tell them to

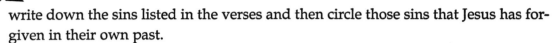

write down the sins listed in the verses and then circle those sins that Jesus has forgiven in their own past.

Read Mark 11:25. Ask group members to privately list anyone that they need to forgive and then pray silently asking God to give them the power to forgive others. Then, have everyone write a brief prayer thanking Jesus for forgiving sin.

PURSUING GOD (5 MINUTES)

NEXT STEPS I NEED TO TAKE

Objective: To take a realistic assessment of one's relationship with Jesus and how that relationship might grow closer in the coming week.

As God's Servant, Jesus continually ministered to the needs of others. Have the group members help you make a list of the needs and concerns of group members, the church and the community. Then ask each person to share one step they need to take to be a more effective servant of the Lord.

With the group, discuss how the needs that you have listed can be met. If possible, choose a service project the group can do together to minister to someone on the list.

PRAYER (5 MINUTES)

Objective: To commit to prayer the listed concerns for service and ministry.

Have the group form a prayer circle. Invite volunteers to lead in prayer focusing on the various needs that were listed on the board. As the leader, close the group in prayer asking God for the power and willingness to serve others in Jesus' name.

Session 3 Bible *Tuck-In*™

UNDERSTANDING MARK

The purpose of this session is:

- To provide an overview of the Gospel of Mark;
- To discover how Jesus Christ is revealed in Mark as the Servant of God.

KEY VERSES

"For even the Son of Man did not come to be served, but to serve, and to give his life as a ransom for many.'" Mark 10:45

"Jesus went into Galilee, proclaiming the good news of God. 'The time has come,' he said. 'The kingdom of God is near. Repent and believe the good news!'" Mark 1:14,15

"'For whoever wants to save his life will lose it, but whoever loses his life for me and for the gospel will save it.'" Mark 8:35

SECTION ONE: GOD'S STORY IN MARK

GOD'S STORY IN MARK

- Greet everyone as they arrive. Tell the story in Mark, doing the suggested activities as you come to them. Distribute the handout "God's Story in Mark" to group members.

Only God's Messiah has the authority to forgive sin and the power to heal the sick.

- Give everyone a pencil or pen and a piece of paper. Ask everyone to turn to Mark 7:20-23. Explain that this is a list of sins that Jesus gave. Tell them to write down the sins listed in the verses and then circle those sins that Jesus has forgiven in their own past.

- Read Mark 11:25,26. Ask group members to privately list anyone that they need to forgive and then pray silently asking God to give them the power to forgive others. Then have everyone write a brief prayer thanking Jesus for forgiving sin.

PURSUING GOD (5 MINUTES)

NEXT STEPS I NEED TO TAKE

- As God's Servant, Jesus continually ministered to the **needs of others.** Have the group members help you make a list of the needs and concerns of group members, the church and the community. Then ask each person to share one step they need to take to be a more effective servant of the Lord.

- With the group, discuss how the needs that you have listed can be met. If possible, choose a service project the group can do together to minister to someone on the list.

PRAYER (5 MINUTES)

- Form a prayer circle. Invite volunteers to lead in prayer focusing on the various needs that were listed on the board.

As the leader, close the group in prayer asking God for the power and willingness to serve others in Jesus' name.

OPTION ONE: (FOR A 90-MINUTE SESSION)

Parables about the Seeds (15 Minutes)

- Ask everyone to follow along in their Bibles as you read Mark 4:1-20. Discuss:
  Why won't seeds grow on hard ground?
  What would make it possible for the seeds to grow?
  How can we best prepare our hearts for receiving the seed of God's Word?
  Where do we need to be sowing God's seed?

- Now read Mark 4:26-29 to the group. Show the group an apple. Ask group members to guess how many seeds are in the apple and write down their estimates on the back of their handouts. Cut open the apple, count the seeds and see who came closest to guessing the correct amount. Then ask, **How many apples are in a seed? Of course, no one knows that answer but God.** Discuss the parable.

- Finally, read Mark 4:30-32. Give each group member a mustard seed (or similar small seed). Have them silently consider how this small seed can grow into such a large plant. Ask for volunteers to share about a time when a small seed of faith in God produced a great blessing or harvest in their lives.

SECTION TWO: GOD'S PERSON (15 MINUTES)

JESUS: THE SERVANT AT PRAYER

- Read Mark 1:35 and 14:32-40.
- Write the titles on the board, flip chart or overhead.
- Ask the group to help you list appropriate answers under each topic. Invite two or three to share testimonies of times

when they prayed and God gave them strength to face a difficult time in life.

- Read Mark 9:17-29, then discuss:
  What kinds of situations require intense prayer and fasting?
  Why do we neglect prayer before we move ahead in tough situations?
  What can we learn from Jesus praying before He faced the cross?

OPTION TWO: (FOR A 90-MINUTE SESSION)

The Servant of God in Power and Authority (15 Minutes)

- Divide the whole group into three groups. Assign each group one chapter from Mark 6—8. Give instructions about forming frozen pictures.

- After five to seven minutes, have each group present their picture and have the rest of the groups try to guess the story. After all three stories have been portrayed, discuss:
  In what ways did these stories portray the authority and power of Jesus?
  Why did those around Jesus have such a difficult time understanding who He was?
  Would we have reacted any differently? Why or why not?

SECTION THREE: GOD'S SON (15 MINUTES)

JESUS CHRIST REVEALED AS THE SERVANT WHO FORGIVES

- Have everyone read Mark 2:1-12. Say: **In Greek, the word *sozo* means both to save and to heal. In this story, Jesus heals the man of both his sin and his physical affliction.**

GOD'S STORY IN MARK

1. Mark is the shortest Gospel. It contains 16 chapters and only 4 parables and it portrays Jesus as the perfect Servant of God.

   Notes:

2. The Servant Prepared (Mark 1:1-13)

   Notes:

   Jesus was prepared by:
   1.
   2.
   3.
   4.
   5.

3. The Servant Working (Mark 1:14—8:30)

   Notes:

   Jesus demonstrated power and authority over...
   Mark 1:21-28 _____
   Mark 1:29-31 _____
   Mark 1:32-34 _____
   Mark 1:40-45 _____
   Mark 2:1-12 _____
   Mark 3:1-5 _____
   Mark 3:6-12 _____

CONTINUED

Mark 4:35-41 _____

Mark 5:1-15 _____

Mark 5:21-34 _____

Mark 5:35-43 _____

Mark 6:45-51 _____

Mark 6:53-56 _____

Mark 7:31-37 _____

Mark 8:1-9 _____

Mark 8:22-26 _____

4. The Servant Rejected (Mark 8:31—15:47)

Notes:

5. The Servant Exalted (Mark 16:1-20)

Notes:

Before the next session, read:

Sunday: The Man "Made [to Be Like] His Brethren" (Luke 1:1—3:38)

Monday: The Man "Tempted...As We Are" (Luke 4:1—8:3)

Tuesday: The Man "Touched with...Our Infirmities" (Luke 8:4—12:48)

Wednesday: The Man "About My Father's Business" (Luke 12:49—16:31)

Thursday: The Man "Never a Man Spoke Like This Man" (Luke 17:1—19:27)

Friday: The Man, Our Kinsman-Redeemer (Luke 19:28—23:56)

Saturday: The Man in Resurrection Glory (Luke 24:1-53)

Understanding Luke

The purpose of this session is:

- To provide an overview of the Gospel of Luke;
- To discover how Jesus Christ is revealed in Luke as the Son of Man.

In this session, group members will learn:

- Key truths about God's story in Luke;
- How Jesus is revealed as the Son of Man;
- The basic principle that Jesus was the only perfect human being, yet He died as an unblemished sacrifice for our sins;
- How to apply the truths revealed in Luke to their daily lives.

KEY VERSES

"And Jesus grew in wisdom and stature, and in favor with God and men." Luke 2:52

"'If anyone would come after me, he must deny himself and take up his cross daily and follow me.'" Luke 9:23

"'I tell you, whoever acknowledges me before men, the Son of Man will also acknowledge him before the angels of God.'" Luke 12:8

"'The Son of Man must be delivered into the hands of sinful men, be crucified and on the third day be raised again.'" Luke 24:7

BEFORE THE SESSION

- Pray for group members by name, asking the Holy Spirit to teach the spiritual truths in Luke to them.
- Read chapter 30 in *What the Bible Is All About*.
- Prepare copies of Session 4 handout "God's Story in Luke" for all group members.
- Check off these supplies once you have secured them:

  ___ A chalkboard and chalk or flip chart or overhead projector with markers.

  ___ Extra Bibles, pencils and paper for group members.

  ___ Three 3x5 cards with each one of them having one of the following Scripture references written on it: Luke 15:1-7; Luke 15:8-10; Luke 15:11-32.

  ___ Three sheets of newsprint, masking tape and felt-tip pens.

- If you are having a 90-minute session, carefully read the two option sections right now and pull together any supplies you need for them.
- Read the entire session and look up every passage. Have your Bible *Tuck-In*™ page ready.
- Arrive early and be ready to warmly greet each group member as he or she arrives.
- Memorize the key verses. Share them periodically and ask the group to repeat them as you teach the session.

SECTION ONE: GOD'S STORY (20 MINUTES)

GOD'S STORY IN LUKE

Objective: To tell God's story so that Christians will apply the truths in Luke in their own lives.

Greet everyone as they arrive. Tell the following story, doing the suggested activities as you come to them. Distribute the handout "God's Story in Luke" to group members.

The Preparation of the Son of Man

Luke wrote the historical account of the man Jesus. Unlike Matthew's focus on Jesus as King, Luke portrays Christ's manhood as perfect and holy (see Luke 1:35). Jesus was born of Mary, raised by Mary and Joseph and grew up normally "in favor with God and men" (Luke 2:51,52).

With the whole group discuss:

What are some of the everyday details of living human life that Luke mentions in chapters 1-2? (The attention given to the details of the government situation; the details about Zechariah's disbelief and Elizabeth's pregnancy; Mary's worry about being pregnant before being married to Joseph; Mary and Joseph having to go to Bethlehem for taxes; all the earthly details of Jesus' birth in the stable; the presentation of Jesus at the Temple; Jesus getting lost from his parents in Jerusalem.)

How does the genealogy of Jesus in Luke 3:23-38 emphasize His humanity? (Luke's geneology goes all the way back to the first man, Adam, rather than just beginning with King David.)

The Ministry of the Son of Man

Luke detailed three parts of Jesus' ministry—His ministry in Galilee (see Luke 4:14—9:50); in Judea (see 9:51—19:27); and in Jerusalem (see 19:28—24:53). As a man, Jesus was rejected in His hometown of Nazareth (see 4:28-30) where He announced His ministry to set free the captives and bring healing and good news to the poor and brokenhearted. Jesus proclaimed the gospel to all humanity, including Gentiles, which angered the Jewish leaders who taught that God's favor and blessing was only for them (see Luke 4:14-36). Jesus ministered through healing and teaching. He called and commissioned His disciples.

Ask everyone to read through Luke 4:14-30, and then discuss the following:

How did Jesus describe His ministry?

To whom was Jesus sent to minister?

Why did so many of the Jewish people become angry with Jesus?

The Son of Man Healed the Sick.

Jesus demonstrates the good news of God by healing the sick and driving out evil spirits (see Luke 4:31-44).

Divide the group into three groups and assign the following passages:

Group One: Luke 5:17-26
Group Two: Luke 7:11-17
Group Three: Luke 8:40-56

Ask each group to answer the following questions about their assigned passage:

How does Jesus demonstrate the power of the Son of Man?

How is He treated by the Scribes and Pharisees? By ordinary Jewish people? By Gentiles?

Have the small groups share their answers with the whole group.

The Son of Man Taught About Living in God's Kingdom.

Jesus was often questioned by the Jewish authorities about His ministry. He used parables and His answers to their questions to teach about God's Kingdom (see Luke 6).

Have the same three groups each read Luke 5:33-39; 7:36-50; 12:13-21 and discuss: **What do these parables teach us about God's Kingdom?**

The Son of Man Commissioned His Disciples to Spread the Good News.

Jesus sent out His disciples to minister to the surrounding countryside (see Luke 9:1-9; 10:1-24).

Read Luke 9:1-9 and then discuss with the whole group what difficulties they believed the disciples faced when they went out to minister in Jesus' name. Then read Luke 9:37-50 and discuss:

How is the commissioning of the disciples similar to Jesus sending us out today to share the gospel? How is it different?

The Suffering of the Son of Man

Only in Luke is the Last Supper personalized (see Luke 22:19,20) when Jesus said, "This cup is the new covenant in my blood, which is poured out for you" (Luke 22:20). Luke also told about the angel who ministered to Jesus in the Garden of Gethsemane and gave the Gentile name of Golgotha—Calvary. While he omits much of what Matthew and Mark wrote about the crucifixion, Luke did record Jesus' final prayer in Luke 23:46.

Read Luke 23:44-49 to the group. Identify how the people mentioned—a Gentile, the women and the masses—responded to Jesus' death.

The Victory of the Son of Man

God raised the Son of Man from the dead. The risen Lord spoke to His disciples on the Emmaus road much the same way that He taught them before His death and resurrection. The Son of Man appeared as the resurrected Christ wherever He chose to verify His resurrection to His followers and then He ascended into heaven (see Luke 24:51).

Have group members read through Luke 24 and find the verses that demonstrate that the risen Lord is the same as the real man Jesus (Luke 24:15,19,30-32,35,36,39,40,42,43,46,47). Discuss why the risen Christ was careful to identify Himself to the disciples.

OPTION ONE: (FOR A 90-MINUTE SESSION)

Go and Do Likewise (15 Minutes)

Ask everyone to read silently as you read aloud the parable of the Good Samaritan in Luke 10:25-37. Divide the group into three small groups. With the whole group brainstorm what modern-day setting this parable could have. For example: A person on the side of the highway whose car has broken down and has been beaten unconscious and robbed by a person who pretended to stop to help. You arrive on the scene. What would you do? Using the contemporary setting, give each group the following assignments:

Group 1: The Samaritan Group—Make two lists. One list is **"Reasons not to stop and help."** List two is **"Reasons to stop and help."** Decide what the determining factor would be in stopping to help.

Group 2: The Religious Group—Make two lists: One list is **"Reasons not to stop and help."** List two is **"Reasons to stop and help."** Decide what the determining factor would be in not stopping to help.

Group 3: The Victim—Make two lists: One list is **"Reasons to be glad someone is stopping to help."** List two is **"Reasons to resist help from a stranger—especially a person from a different background."** Decide what the determining factor would be in accepting help.

After all three groups have completed their lists, ask them to share. Discuss:
How is Jesus like the Good Samaritan?
What does He expect of us?
What keeps us from "doing likewise"?

SECTION TWO: GOD'S PERSON (15 MINUTES)

THE DISCIPLE: THE COST OF FOLLOWING JESUS
Objective: To discover how Jesus calls disciples to follow Him.

Luke records the calling of the twelve disciples and how Jesus called others to follow Him. Jesus described a disciple and the cost of discipleship. In the same three groups, assign one of the following passages to each group to read: Luke 5:1-11,27-32; 6:12-16; 9:23-27 and find the answer to the following: **What does it cost personally to become a disciple of Jesus Christ?** Give them about five minutes to read their assignments and complete their discussions.

Give each group a sheet of newsprint and felt-tip pens. Ask them to write the following heading on their newsprint: **"Being a disciple is ...."** Then have them list as many things from their assigned passage as they can to complete the statement.

After about five minutes, ask the groups to put their newsprint sheets up on the walls and then to share briefly with the whole group what they listed.

OPTION TWO: (FOR A 90-MINUTE SESSION)

Who Is the Son of Man? (15 Minutes)

Assign each of the following verses to various group members. If there are not enough passages for everyone, then some can work in pairs. Ask them to look up their verse(s), read to find out how He is described and then complete the following sentence: **The Son of Man is...**

Assign the following passages:

Luke 5:24 (able to forgive sins)

Luke 6:5 (Lord of the Sabbath)

Luke 7:34 (human, friend of sinners)

Luke 9:22 (going to suffer, be rejected, killed and raised from death)

Luke 9:58 (homeless)

Luke 12:40 (coming again)

Luke 18:8,31 (prophecies will be fulfilled)

Luke 19:10 (came to seek the lost)

Luke 21:27 (returning with power and great glory)

Luke 22:22 (betrayed)

Luke 22:69 (seated at the right hand of God)

Luke 24:7 (to be crucified and raised on the third day)

As each person shares what he or she has discovered, write it down on the board. Once everyone has reported, discuss:

What is the most difficult saying Jesus made about the Son of Man?

Why was the Son of Man rejected by many of the Jewish people?

What does calling Jesus "the Son of Man" mean to us today?

SECTION THREE: GOD'S SON (15 MINUTES)

JESUS CHRIST REVEALED IN LUKE'S PARABLES

Objective: To see how Jesus is revealed as the one seeking to save the lost in Luke's parables.

Read Luke 5:31,32 to the group. Say: **The physician Luke gives us great insights about the Great Physician, Jesus. Only the sick need to be healed. Only the guilty need to repent. Only the lost need to be found. Luke records three parables about finding and saving the lost for the Kingdom of God.**

Have the members return to the same three groups. Give each group a 3x5-inch card with the Scripture reference for the parable they will mime for the whole group. Everyone else is to try to guess what parable is being presented. The parables are:

The Lost Sheep—Luke 15:1-7
The Lost Coin—Luke 15:8-10
The Lost Son—Luke 15:11-32

After the presentations, discuss:

How important are the lost to God?

What is heaven's response when the lost are found or saved?

What did Jesus do to reach out to the lost?

What attitude would Jesus have us possess toward the lost?

PURSUING GOD (5 MINUTES)

NEXT STEPS I NEED TO TAKE

Objective: To take a realistic assessment of one's relationship with Jesus and how that relationship might grow closer in the coming week.

Ask group members to find a partner. Invite the pairs to fill out the "Cost of Discipleship" section on their handouts and then share with their partners how they have responded. Ask them to share what the next step is that they need to take to remove any barrier keeping them from fully following Jesus.

PRAYER (5 MINUTES)

Objective: To pray to follow Jesus fully and completely.

In pairs, ask each person to pray for the next step that their partner has identified. Then have the whole group sing "I Surrender All" as a closing prayer or simply say the words of the song in unison.

All to Jesus I surrender;
All to Him I freely give.
I will ever love and trust Him.
In His presence daily live.

I surrender all.
I surrender all.
All to Thee, my blessed Savior,
I surrender all.

Session 4 Bible *Tuck-In*™

UNDERSTANDING LUKE

The purpose of this session is:

- To provide an overview of the Gospel of Luke;
- To discover how Jesus Christ is revealed in Luke as the Son of Man.

KEY VERSES

"And Jesus grew in wisdom and stature, and in favor with God and men." Luke 2:52

"'If anyone would come after me, he must deny himself and take up his cross daily and follow me.'" Luke 9:23

"'I tell you, whoever acknowledges me before men, the Son of Man will also acknowledge him before the angels of God.'" Luke 12:8

"'The Son of Man must be delivered into the hands of sinful men, be crucified and on the third day be raised again.'" Luke 24:7

-------- Fold --------

---

parables of how the Kingdom of God is about finding and saving the lost.

- Have the members return to the same three groups. Give each group a 3x5-inch card with the Scripture reference for the parable they will mime for the whole group. Everyone else is to try to guess what parable is being presented. The parables are: The Lost Sheep—Luke 15:1-7; The Lost Coin—Luke 15:8-10; The Lost Son—Luke 15:11-32.

- After the presentations, discuss:

  How important are the lost to God?

  What is heaven's response when the lost are found or saved?

  What did Jesus do to reach out to the lost?

  What attitude would Jesus have us possess toward the lost?

PURSUING GOD (5 MINUTES)

NEXT STEPS I NEED TO TAKE

- Ask group members to form pairs. Invite the pairs to fill out the "Cost of Discipleship" section on their handouts and then share with their partners how they have responded. Ask them to share what the next step is that they need to take to remove any barrier keeping them from fully following Jesus.

PRAYER (5 MINUTES)

- In pairs, ask each person to pray for the next step that their partner has identified. Then have the whole group sing "I Surrender All" as a closing prayer or simply say the words of the song in unison.

SECTION ONE: GOD'S STORY (20 MINUTES)

GOD'S STORY IN LUKE

- Greet everyone as they arrive. Tell the story in Luke, doing the suggested activities as you come to them. Distribute the handout "God's Story in Luke" to group members.

OPTION ONE: (FOR A 90-MINUTE SESSION)

Go and Do Likewise (15 Minutes)

- Ask everyone to read silently as you read aloud the Parable of the Good Samaritan in Luke 10:25-37. Divide the group into three small groups. With the whole group, brainstorm what modern-day setting this parable could have. Choosing a contemporary Good Samaritan situation, give the three groups their assignments.

- After all three groups have completed their lists, ask them to share their lists with the whole group. Discuss:
  How is Jesus like the Good Samaritan? What does He expect of us?
  What keeps us from "doing likewise"?

SECTION TWO: GOD'S PERSON (15 MINUTES)

THE DISCIPLE: THE COST OF FOLLOWING JESUS

- In the same three groups, assign one of the following passages to each group to read: Luke 5:1-11,27-32; 6:12-16; 9:23-27 and find the answer to: **What does it cost personally to become a disciple of Jesus Christ?** Give them five minutes to do this.

- Give each group a sheet of newsprint and felt-tip pens. Ask them to write the following heading on their newsprint:
  "Being a disciple is..." Then have them list as many things

- - - - - - - - - - Fold - - - - - - - - - -

from their assigned passage as they can to complete the statement.

- After about five minutes, ask the groups to put their newsprint sheets up on the walls and then to share briefly with the whole group what they listed.

OPTION TWO: (FOR A 90-MINUTE SESSION)

Who Is the Son of Man? (15 Minutes)

- Assign each of the sets of verses to different group members. If there are not enough passages for everyone, then have some work together in pairs. Ask them to look up their verse(s) and then to complete the sentence: **The Son of Man is...**

- The passages to be assigned are: Luke 5:24; 6:5; 7:34; 9:22; 9:58; 12:40; 18:31; 19:10; 21:27; 22:22; 22:69; 24:7.

- As each person shares what he or she has discovered, write it down on the board. Once everyone has reported, discuss:
  What is the most difficult saying Jesus made about the Son of Man?
  Why was the Son of Man rejected by the Jews?
  What does calling Jesus "the Son of Man" mean to us today?

SECTION THREE: GOD'S SON (15 MINUTES)

JESUS CHRIST REVEALED IN LUKE'S PARABLES

- Read Luke 5:31,32 to the group. Say: The physician Luke gives us great insights about the Great Physician, Jesus. Only the sick need healing. Only the guilty need repenting. Only the lost need finding. Luke records three

GOD'S STORY IN LUKE

1. The Preparation of the Son of Man

   Notes:

2. The Ministry of the Son of Man

   Notes:

3. The Son of Man Healed the Sick

   Notes:

4. The Son of Man Taught God's Ways

   Notes:

5. The Son of Man Commissioned His Disciples to Spread the Good News

   Notes:

CONTINUED

6. The Suffering of the Son of Man

Notes:

7. The Victory of the Son of Man

Notes:

THE COST OF DISCIPLESHIP
In order to follow Jesus, which of the following are the most difficult for you to surrender or release:
(Check any that may apply.)
❑ Unbelieving family members
❑ Sinful or destructive relationships
❑ Material wealth/possessions
❑ Work entanglements
❑ Personal goals for success
❑ Religious attitudes of legalism or traditionalism
❑ Sin habits
❑ Pleasures that I enjoy that keep me from worship and serving God
❑ Other: _____

Before the next session, read:
Sunday: Christ Became Flesh (John 1:1-51)
Monday: Christ So Loved (John 3:1-36)
Tuesday: Christ Satisfies (John 4:1-54)
Wednesday: Christ, the Bread of Life (John 6:1-59)
Thursday: Christ, the Light of the World (John 9:1-41)
Friday: Christ, Our Shepherd (John 10:1-39)
Saturday: Christ Promises the Comforter (John 14:1-31)

Understanding John

The purpose of this session is:

- To provide an overview of the Gospel of John;
- To discover how Jesus Christ is revealed in John as the Son of God.

In this session, group members will learn:

- Key truths about God's story in John;
- That Jesus Christ is revealed as the Son of God;
- The basic principle that the signs and wonders recorded in John demonstrate the deity of Jesus;
- How to apply the truths revealed in John to their daily lives.

KEY VERSES

"The Word became flesh and made his dwelling among us. We have seen his glory, the glory of the One and Only, who came from the Father, full of grace and truth." John 1:14

"Jesus answered, 'I am the way and the truth and the life. No one comes to the Father except through me.'" John 14:6

"'Greater love has no one than this, that he lay down his life for his friends. You are my friends if you do what I command.'" John 15:13,14

"But these are written that you may believe that Jesus is the Christ, the Son of God, and that by believing you may have life in his name." John 20:31

BEFORE THE SESSION

- Pray for group members by name, asking the Holy Spirit to reveal to them the spiritual truths in John.
- Read chapter 31 in *What the Bible Is All About*.
- Prepare copies of the Session 5 handout "God's Story in John" for group members.
- Check off these supplies once you have secured them:
  - _____ A chalkboard and chalk or flip chart or overhead projector with markers.
  - _____ Extra Bibles, pencils and paper for group members.
  - _____ Before the session, contact a husband and wife or your spouse or a friend

of yours and arrange to have the husband prepared to wash the feet of his wife, or you wash the feet of your spouse or friend. You will need a basin or bowl, a pitcher of water and a towel.

_____ Poster board, felt-tip pens, glue, scissors, magazines and tape for making collages for seven groups.

• If you are having a 90-minute session, carefully read the two option sections right now and pull together any supplies you need for them.

• Read the entire session and look up every passage. Have your Bible *Tuck-In*™ page ready.

• Arrive early and be ready to warmly greet each group member as he or she arrives.

• Memorize the key verses. Share them periodically and ask the group to repeat them as you teach the session.

SECTION ONE: GOD'S STORY (20 MINUTES)

GOD'S STORY IN JOHN
Objective: To tell God's story so that Christians will apply the truths in John in their own lives.

Greet everyone as they arrive. Tell the following story, doing the suggested activities as you come to them. Distribute the handout "God's Story in John" to group members.

The theme of John's Gospel is the deity, or the divine nature, of Jesus Christ. In every chapter He is revealed as deity—the Son of God (see John 1:49).

Assign one or more of the following passages to various group members to read aloud: John 1:49; 2:11; 3:16; 4:26; 5:25; 6:32,33; 7:37; 8:58; 9:37,38; 10:30; 11:27; 12:32; 13:13; 14:1; 15:15; 16:7; 17:1; 18:37; 19:30; 20:28; 21:22. Ask each person to read the passage(s) and then share one aspect that the passage reveals about Jesus being God's Son.

John's Great Prologue (John 1:1-18)

Jesus is revealed as the Word of God becoming flesh so that those who believe in Him will become the children of God (see John 1:12).

Have group members examine John 1:1-18 and call out every description and characteristic of God's Word. List those characteristics on the board, flip chart or overhead. Then discuss:

Which of these characteristics are also qualities of God?

How is Jesus' divine nature revealed in this passage?

Jesus' Public Ministry (John 1:19—12:50)

John may be called the Gospel of Signs. A "sign" is a miracle performed by Jesus to demonstrate His deity and point to His glory so that people might believe in Him (see John 2:11).

Divide the whole group into seven smaller groups. Assign each small group one of the following signs in John. Ask each group to describe that sign in one sentence and to point out how that sign demonstrated the deity of Jesus.

John 2:1-11 (Turning water into wine)

John 4:46-54 (Healing the nobleman's son)

John 5:1-14 (Healing the man at the Pool of Bethesda)

John 6:5-14 (Feeding the 5,000)

John 6:16-21 (Walking on water)

John 9:1-33 (Healing the blind man)

John 11:1-44 (Raising of Lazarus)

Jesus' Private Ministry (John 13—17)

During Jesus' last week, He taught His disciples and cleansed the Temple. When Jesus washed His disciples feet, He demonstrated a lesson in servanthood (see John 13:1-11).

As previously arranged, have a husband wash his wife's feet or you wash your spouse's or friend's feet. Have the person washing feet share how he or she feels. Then have the person whose feet are washed share his or her feelings. Discuss with the whole group:

What do you think the disciples must have been thinking and feeling while Jesus washed their feet?

How would you have felt?

What spiritual principles was Jesus teaching with this demonstration?

Jesus' Suffering and Death (John 18—19)

Betrayed by Judas and deserted by His disciples, Jesus was tried before the High Priest and Pilate. Being sentenced to death by Pilate, Jesus was crucified at

Golgotha between two criminals (see John 19:18). **He took care of His mother (see vv. 26,27), spoke of His thirst (see vv. 28,29) and then pronounced: "It is finished"** (v. 30).

Divide the whole group into four groups and assign each group one of the following passages:

Group One: Matthew 27:33-46
Group Two: Mark 15:22-34
Group Three: Luke 23:32-43
Group Four: John 19:17-30

Ask each group to read its assigned passage and to write down the words Jesus uttered while He was on the cross. Then have all the groups report back and write on the board, flip chart or overhead the seven last sayings of Jesus on the cross. Have the small groups share which words are most meaningful to each person in the small group and why.

Jesus' Victory over Death (John 20—21)

God raised Jesus from the dead. Jesus appeared to Mary Magdalene, then to the ten disciples and finally to Thomas. Jesus met and ate with His disciples in Galilee and forgave Peter (see John 21:15-25).

Do a dramatic reading of John 20. Assign the following parts:

A narrator
Mary Magdalene
Jesus
Thomas

After the reading, discuss the following:
What surprises you about the way the disciples responded to the risen Jesus? Do you identify with Thomas? Why or why not?

OPTION ONE: (FOR A 90-MINUTE SESSION)

I Believe (15 Minutes)

Have the group members form pairs. Say: **This activity is a witnessing exercise. The older partner gets to go first. That person will say, "I believe in God." The partner will ask, "Why?" That person will respond with a simple, one-sentence statement like, "Because when I see creation, I believe a Creator God must have**

created everything." Then the partner will ask, "Why?" After every statement will come the same question, "Why?" After one minute, have the partners switch roles and the other partner says, "I believe that Jesus is the Son of God." That person is asked, "Why?" Continue that dialogue for one minute. I will call time after each minute. Go.

After both partners have shared, discuss with the whole group:

What was difficult with this dialogue?

How did you feel when you were trying to give answers?

Now read John 8:42-59 and discuss:

How did the Jews feel toward Jesus and His answers?

Were they frustrated in the same way some of us became frustrated?

Was there any answer Jesus could have given that might have satisfied the Jews?

What do you believe to be the ultimate proof of Jesus' deity?

If someone does not believe that Jesus is the Son of God, how would you answer his or her questions about Him?

SECTION TWO: GOD'S PERSON (15 MINUTES)

WITNESSES TO JESUS IN JOHN'S GOSPEL

Ask group members who wish to share a brief witness of how they know that Jesus Christ is God's Son. Say: **A witness—*martus* in the Greek—is one who gives evidence or who testifies that something has really happened. John used this same language of the courtroom to describe what the disciples had experienced firsthand—the resurrection of Christ** (see John 20:25; 21:24). **Share one way you have seen the risen Lord in your life.**

After everyone shares, say: **John is careful to produce important, reliable witnesses to the truth that Jesus is God's son. Six eyewitnesses in addition to Jesus Himself are witnesses to His deity.**

Assign the following passages to various group members to be read to the whole group: John 1:34; 1:49; 6:68,69; 11:27; 20:28; 20:31.

After these passages about witnesses have been read, discuss:

What makes an eyewitness credible or believable?

Who were the most important witnesses in your life about the deity of Jesus?

How did they witness to you about the risen Lord?

OPTION TWO: (FOR A 90-MINUTE SESSION)

Jesus Sends the Holy Spirit (15 Minutes)

Have the whole group brainstorm everything they know about the Holy Spirit as you write their suggestions on the board, flip chart or overhead.

Divide the group into three groups. Have each group read one of the following passages about the Holy Spirit and then write a short description of the Holy Spirit: John 14:15-30; John 15:26,27; John 16:5-16.

Have the groups share their descriptions of the Holy Spirit. After every group has shared, invite anyone who wishes to share how the Holy Spirit has ministered in his or her life.

SECTION THREE: GOD'S SON (15 MINUTES)

JESUS CHRIST REVEALED AS THE SON OF GOD

Objective: To discover how Jesus reveals Himself to be deity—the "I Am"—in the Gospel of John.

Divide the whole group into seven groups. Give each small group felt-tip pens, magazines, glue, tape and a piece of poster board. Assign one of the following passages to each group and instruct them to create a collage representing the "I Am" as described in their assigned Scripture. After all the collages are completed, ask each group to share its collage with the whole group. During the sharing, list each group's "I Am" and its Scripture reference on the board, flip chart or overhead. Invite group members to take notes on their handouts under the section entitled "Jesus Is the I Am."

Group One:	**John 6:35** (I am the bread of life.)
Group Two:	**John 8:12** (I am the light of the world.)
Group Three:	**John 8:58** (Before Abraham was, I am.)
Group Four:	**John 10:11** (I am the good shepherd.)

Group Five:	John 11:25 (I am the resurrection and the life.)
Group Six:	John 14:6 (I am the way and the truth and the life.)
Group Seven:	John 15:1 (I am the true vine.)

PURSUING GOD (5 MINUTES)

NEXT STEPS I NEED TO TAKE

Objective: To take a realistic assessment of one's relationship with Jesus and how that relationship might grow closer in the coming week.

In restoring the relationship between Himself and Peter, Jesus commanded Peter, "Feed my sheep" (John 21:17). What do you believe Jesus wanted Peter to do?

Discuss this for a few minutes, then ask: **What do you believe Jesus would want each of us to do in response to this command? Find a partner and share your completion of the statement, "One way that Jesus would have me feed his sheep is..."**

PRAYER (5 MINUTES)

Objective: To experience the meaning of Jesus' priestly prayer in John 17 as it applies to us and through intercession for other believers.

Ask each person to write a prayer thanking Jesus for His prayer for us in John 17. After writing that prayer of thanksgiving, ask group members to write down one sentence of intercession for all believers similar to the way Jesus prayed for all believers (see John 17:20-26).

Close the session with volunteers reading their one-sentence prayers of intercession.

Session 5 Bible *Tuck-In*™

UNDERSTANDING JOHN

The purpose of this session is:

- To provide an overview of the Gospel of John;
- To discover how Jesus Christ is revealed in John as the Son of God.

KEY VERSES

"The Word became flesh and made his dwelling among us. We have seen his glory, the glory of the One and Only, who came from the Father, full of grace and truth." John 1:14

"Jesus answered, 'I am the way and the truth and the life. No one comes to the Father except through me.'" John 14:6

"'Greater love has no one than this, that he lay down his life for his friends. You are my friends if you do what I command.'" John 15:13,14

"But these are written that you may believe that Jesus is the Christ, the Son of God, and that by believing you may have life in his name." John 20:31

---

sharing, list each group's "I Am" and its Scripture reference on the board, flip chart or overhead. Invite them to take notes on their handouts under the section entitled "Jesus Is the I Am."

Group One:	John 6:35 (I am the bread of life.)
Group Two:	John 8:12 (I am the light of the world.)
Group Three:	John 8:58 (Before Abraham was, I am.)
Group Four:	John 10:11 (I am the good shepherd.)
Group Five:	John 11:25 (I am the resurrection and the life.)
Group Six:	John 14:6 (I am the way, truth and life.)
Group Seven:	John 15:1 (I am the true vine.)

PURSUING GOD (5 MINUTES)

NEXT STEPS I NEED TO TAKE

- **In restoring the relationship between Himself and Peter, Jesus commanded Peter, "Feed my sheep" (John 21:17). What do you believe Jesus wanted Peter to do?**

- Discuss this for a few minutes, then ask: **What do you believe Jesus would want each of us to do in response to this command? Find a partner and share your completion of the statement, "One way that Jesus would have me feed his sheep is..."**

PRAYER (5 MINUTES)

- Ask each person to write a prayer thanking Jesus for His prayer for us in John 17. After writing that prayer of thanksgiving, ask group members to write down one sentence of intercession for all believers similar to the way Jesus prayed for all believers (see John 17:20-26).

- Close the session with volunteers reading their one-sentence prayers of intercession.

SECTION ONE: GOD'S STORY (20 MINUTES)

GOD'S STORY IN JOHN

- Greet everyone as they arrive. Tell the story in John, doing the suggested activities as you come to them. Distribute the handout "God's Story in John" to group members.

OPTION ONE: (FOR A 90-MINUTE SESSION)

I Believe (15 Minutes)

- Have the group form pairs. Give instructions on the witnessing activity. After the partners have shared, discuss:
  What was difficult with this dialogue?
  How did you feel when you were trying to give answers?
- Read John 8:42-59, then discuss:
  How did the Jews feel toward Jesus and His answers?
  Were they becoming frustrated in the same way some of us became frustrated?
  Was there any answer Jesus could have given that might have satisfied the Jews?
  What do you believe to be the ultimate proof of Jesus' deity?
  If someone does not believe that Jesus is the Son of God, how would you answer his or her questions about Him?

SECTION TWO: GOD'S PERSON (15 MINUTES)

WITNESSES TO JESUS IN JOHN'S GOSPEL

- Ask each person in the group to share a brief witness of how they know that Jesus Christ is God's Son. Say: A witness—*martus* in the Greek—is one who gives evidence or testifies that something has really happened. John used this same language of the courtroom to describe

74

------ Fold ------

what the disciples had experienced firsthand—the resurrection of Christ (see John 20:25; 21:24).

- Assign the following seven passages to be read out loud: John 1:34; 1:49; 6:68,69; 11:27; 20:28; 20:31. After these passages about witnesses have been read, discuss:
  What makes an eyewitness credible or believable?
  Who were the most important witnesses in your life about the deity of Jesus?
  How did they witness to you about the risen Lord?

OPTION TWO: (FOR A 90-MINUTE SESSION)

Jesus Sends the Holy Spirit (15 Minutes)

- Have the whole group brainstorm everything they know about the Holy Spirit as you write their suggestions on the board, flip chart or overhead.
- Divide the group into three groups. Have each group read one of the passages about the Holy Spirit and then write a short description of the Holy Spirit: John 14:15-30; John 15:26,27; John 16:5-16.
- Have the groups share their descriptions of the Holy Spirit. After every group has shared, invite anyone who wishes to share how the Holy Spirit has ministered in his or her life.

SECTION THREE: GOD'S SON (15 MINUTES)

JESUS CHRIST REVEALED AS THE SON OF GOD

- Divide the whole group into seven groups. Give each small group felt-tip pens, magazines, glue, tape and a sheet of poster board. Assign one of the following passages to each group and instruct them to create a collage representing the "I Am" in their assigned Scripture. Ask each group to share its completed collage with the whole group. During the

GOD'S STORY IN JOHN

1. The theme of John's gospel is the deity of Jesus Christ. In every chapter He is revealed as deity—the Son of God (see John 1:49).

   Notes:

2. John's Great Prologue (John 1:1-18)

   Notes:

3. Jesus' Public Ministry (John 1:19—12:50)

   Notes:

4. Jesus' Private Ministry (John 13—17)

   Notes:

5. Jesus' Suffering and Death (John 18—19)

   Notes:

CONTINUED

6. Jesus' Victory over Death (John 20—21)

Notes:

JESUS IS THE I AM
1. _____
2. _____
3. _____
4. _____
5. _____
6. _____
7. _____

Before the next session, read:
Sunday: Power in the Early Church (Acts 2)
Monday: Justified by Faith (Romans 5)
Tuesday: The Body of Christ (1 Corinthians 12)
Wednesday: The Head of the Church (Ephesians 1)
Thursday: Living in the Spirit (Romans 8; Galatians 5)
Friday: Joyful Living (Philippians 4)
Saturday: Christ, Lord of All (Colossians 1:15-23)

Previewing Acts Through Philippians

The purpose of this session is:

- To provide an overview of Acts through Philippians;
- To discover how Jesus Christ is revealed in these New Testament books as Lord of the Church.

In this session, group members will learn:

- Key truths about God's story in the early church;
- That Jesus is revealed as Lord of the Church;
- The basic principles that Christ is leading His bride, the Church, into the future and preparing her for His return;
- How to apply the truths revealed in these books to their daily lives.

KEY VERSES

"They devoted themselves to the apostles' teaching and to the fellowship, to the breaking of bread and to prayer. Everyone was filled with awe, and many wonders and miraculous signs were done by the apostles." Acts 2:42,43

"For it is by grace you have been saved, through faith—and this not from yourselves, it is the gift of God—not by works, so that no one can boast." Ephesians 2:8,9

"Speak to one another with psalms, hymns and spiritual songs. Sing and make music in your heart to the Lord, always giving thanks to God the Father for everything, in the name of our Lord Jesus Christ." Ephesians 5:19,20

BEFORE THE SESSION

- Pray for group members by name, asking the Holy Spirit to reveal to them the spiritual truths in these books.
- Prepare copies of Session 6 handout "God's Story in Acts Through Philippians."
- Check off these supplies once you have secured them:
  - _____ A chalkboard and chalk or flip chart or overhead projector with markers.
  - _____ Extra Bibles, pencils and paper for group members.

_____ A good map of the New Testament world would be helpful to see the cities where Paul and the other apostles went to establish churches.

_____ Write each of the following Scripture references on separate 3x5-inch index cards: Romans 1:16; 3:23; 5:1; 8:1; 12:1,2; 13:8-10; 1 Corinthians 13:1-8; 15:56-58; 2 Corinthians 3:18; 5:7,17; 8:9; 9:7; Galatians 5:22; 6:7; Ephesians 2:8.

_____ Sheets of newsprint and felt-tip pens.

- If you are having a 90-minute session, carefully read the two option sections right now and pull together any supplies you need for them.

- Read the entire session and look up every passage. Have your Bible _Tuck-In_™ page ready.

- Arrive early and be ready to warmly greet each group member as he or she arrives.

- Memorize the key verses. Share them periodically and ask the group to repeat them as you teach the session.

SECTION ONE: GOD'S STORY (20 MINUTES)

GOD'S STORY IN ACTS THROUGH PHILIPPIANS

Objective: To tell God's story so that Christians will apply the truths in these books to their own lives.

Greet everyone as they arrive. Tell the following story, doing the suggested activities as you come to them. Distribute the handout "God's Story in Acts Through Philippians" to the group members.

Jesus sent the Holy Spirit to empower the Early Church to become His witnesses in Jerusalem, Judea, Samaria and the whole earth (see Acts 1:8).

The Holy Spirit was poured out at Pentecost (see Acts 2:1-4) **giving boldness to the early Christians to witness with power about Jesus as the risen Lord and Savior and to minister with signs and wonders in the name of Jesus** (see Acts 2:42-47; 5:12-16).

Read Acts 2:42-47. Have the group brainstorm all the types of ministry and worship occurring in the Early Church and list on the board, flip chart or overhead.

Then discuss:
Which of these qualities of the Early Church do we see today?
Which ones do we not see today? Why not?
How can we experience God's power more like the Early Church did?

God converted the Jewish persecutor of the early Church—Saul—into the missionary Paul to take the gospel message to the Gentiles throughout the Mediterranean world.

Paul went on missionary journeys throughout the Roman empire to plant churches in Asia Minor, Greece and finally in Rome, where he was imprisoned and martyred (see Acts 13:4—14:28; 15:39—18:22; 18:23—21:17; 27:1—28:16).

Divide the group into four smaller groups. Assign each group one of the following passages: Acts 13:4—14:28; 15:39—18:22; 18:23—21:17; 27:1—28:16. Ask each group to skim their passage and summarize what happened to Paul during that journey and report back to the whole group. Discuss:
In what ways do missionaries today face similar dangers?
How is being a missionary different today?

Paul wrote letters to churches throughout the known world to address problems and conflicts, to teach truth, combat heresy and encourage the new converts to Christianity.

Early in his ministry, he wrote to the Thessalonians and Galatians. Later he wrote to the churches in Corinth, Ephesus, Colosse, Rome, Philippi and to his friend, Philemon (see 1 Thessalonians 1:1; 2 Thessalonians 1:1; Galatians 1:1-5; 1 Corinthians 1:2; 2 Corinthians 1:1; Ephesians 1:1-3; Colossians 1:1,2; Romans 1:1-7; Philippians 1:1,2; Philemon 1).

Discuss the following:
If Paul were writing letters to the Church in America, what kinds of issues and problems might he address today?
What kinds of communications do church leaders use today to help local churches learn God's Word and work through problems?

After Paul's release from prison in A.D. 62-63, he traveled on his fourth missionary journey and wrote the "pastoral epistles" of 1 and 2 Timothy and Titus.

They were in pastoral ministry and needed guidance and direction in shepherding their congregations (see 1 Timothy 1:1-4; 2 Timothy 1:1,2; Titus 1:1-14).

Discuss with the group:
What are the qualifications in your local church for people entering into the ministry?
What are the central issues facing those entering ministry today?

Paul's letters are filled with many teachings and exhortations.

The two most common themes in his writing are:

1. **We are justified by faith in Jesus Christ who died for our sins and through whom we are saved by grace apart from our own works or efforts** (see Romans 5:1-11; Ephesians 2:1-10).
2. **We are being sanctified by the Holy Spirit to live righteous and holy lives** (see Romans 8; 2 Corinthians 3; Galatians 5).

To see how much our faith has been shaped by Paul's letters, pass out the 3x5-inch index cards on which you have previously written the Scripture references to various group members. Have each Scripture read aloud to the group without the reference and then ask people to raise their hands if they have ever heard that passage before. Ask how many know in what book the passage is found. Many of these passages will be very familiar to the group, which indicates how much Paul's writings have affected today's sermons and teaching.

OPTION ONE: (FOR A 90-MINUTE SESSION)

THE EARLY CHURCH (15 MINUTES)

Throughout the New Testament we can find portraits of life in the Early Church. Divide the group into six small groups. Assign the following Scripture passages to each group. Ask each group to paraphrase their verses as if they were writing a news report. When the groups are finished, have the groups present their passage as part of a local news show and read the reports as if being reported by Headline News. Assign the following passages:

Group One:	Acts 2:1-13, 42-46
Group Two:	Acts 4:31-35
Group Three:	1 Corinthians 11:17-34
Group Four:	Ephesians 5:18-20
Group Five:	1 Corinthians 14:26-28
Group Six:	Colossians 3:15-17

Section Two: God's Person (15 Minutes)

Paul: Missionary to the Gentiles

Objective: To discover how Christ radically changed Saul the persecutor into Paul the missionary and used him in mighty ways for spreading the gospel.

Read Acts 7:57—8:3; 9:1-19 to the group.

Saul experienced a radical conversion experience on the road to Damascus. He was traveling there to imprison and persecute Christians. Let's find out what kinds of conversion experiences we have had in our midst.

Invite volunteers from the group to share their conversion experiences. Especially encourage those who did not grow up in a Christian family or those who greatly disliked Christians or churches to share their conversion experiences. **Saul's conversion led him to travel great distances to share the gospel of Christ.** Discuss: **What are some ways we can share the gospel today?** Make a list on the board as the group shares.

What kinds of persecution and difficulties do Christians face today in sharing the gospel?

Option Two: (For a 90-Minute Session)

Paul: Writer of Epistles (15 Minutes)

Ask everyone to write a letter to someone—real or imagined—in a distant city. The letter should encourage the recipient to follow Jesus and live a holy life. Also send personal greetings to individual family members.

Ask various volunteers to share the letters they have written. Then ask the group members to identify the main element in all of the letters. Write their input on the board. Then say: **Paul's letters, much like ours, have three basic elements— salutary or opening greeting and introduction often containing a prayer; the main**

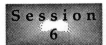

body of the letter and the closing personal comments with a benediction—a final prayer of blessing.

As an example, have everyone turn to 2 Thessalonians. Have the group identify the opening greeting and introduction, the main body of the letter and the closing comments and benediction. Your findings should be:

    Greeting and prayer: 1:1-12.
    Main body of the Epistle: 2—3:15
    Final comments, personal greetings and benediction: 3:16-18

SECTION THREE: GOD'S SON (15 MINUTES)

JESUS CHRIST REVEALED AS LORD OF THE CHURCH

Objective: To see how Jesus is revealed in these books as Lord of the Body of Christ—His Church.

Jesus Christ is the head of His Body, the Church. The Church is not a program, a doctrine or a man. The risen Christ is leading His bride—the Church—into the future and preparing her for His return.

Divide the whole group into four small groups. Give each group a sheet of newsprint and felt-tip pens. Ask each group to list how Christ is the head and leading the Church, according to their assigned text. Ask them to also list ways that they see Jesus leading the local church in light of their texts. After about seven minutes, invite each small group to share what they have written on their newsprint.

    Group One: Ephesians 1:15-23
    Group Two: 1 Corinthians 3:5-23
    Group Three: Ephesians 4:11-16
    Group Four: 1 Corinthians 12:12-31

PURSUING GOD (5 MINUTES)

NEXT STEPS I NEED TO TAKE

Objective: To take a realistic assessment of one's relationship with Jesus and how that relationship might grow closer in the coming week.

Ask everyone to turn to Philippians 4 and read the chapter silently and then choose one favorite verse that challenges them to grow spiritually. Ask everyone to find a partner and share his or her chosen verse and a step that they will take to grow spiritually in the coming week in line with the verse.

PRAYER (5 MINUTES)

Objective: To pray a New Testament prayer for another group member.

Have the pairs turn to Ephesians 3:14-21 and pray this prayer for one another in closing.

Session 6 Bible *Tuck-In*™

PREVIEWING ACTS THROUGH PHILIPPIANS

The purpose of this session is:
- To provide an overview of Acts through Philippians;
- To discover how Jesus Christ is revealed in these New Testament books as Lord of the Church.

KEY VERSES

"They devoted themselves to the apostles' teaching and to the fellowship, to the breaking of bread and to prayer. Everyone was filled with awe, and many wonders and miraculous signs were done by the apostles." Acts 2:42,43

"For it is by grace you have been saved, through faith—and this not from yourselves, it is the gift of God—not by works, so that no one can boast." Ephesians 2:8,9

"Speak to one another with psalms, hymns and spiritual songs. Sing and make music in your heart to the Lord, always giving thanks to God the Father for everything, in the name of our Lord Jesus Christ." Ephesians 5:19,20

---

of their verses. After about seven minutes, invite each small group to share what they have written on their newsprint.

Group One:	Ephesians 1:15-23
Group Two:	1 Corinthians 3:5-23
Group Three:	Ephesians 4:11-16
Group Four:	1 Corinthians 12:12-31

PURSUING GOD (5 MINUTES)

NEXT STEPS I NEED TO TAKE

- Ask everyone to turn to Philippians 4 and read the chapter silently and then choose one favorite verse that challenges them to grow spiritually. Ask everyone to find a partner and share his or her chosen verse and a step that they will take to grow spiritually in the coming week in line with the verse.

PRAYER (5 MINUTES)

- Have the pairs turn to Ephesians 3:14-21 and pray this prayer for one another in closing.

Section One: God's Story (20 Minutes)

God's Story in Acts Through Philippians

- Greet everyone as they arrive. Tell the story of Acts through Philippians, doing the suggested activities as you come to them. Distribute the handout "God's Story in Acts Through Philippians" to all the group members.

Option One: (For a 90-Minute Session)

The Early Church (15 Minutes)

- Divide the group into six small groups. Assign the Scripture passages to each group. Ask each group to paraphrase their verses as if they were writing a news report. When the groups are finished, have the groups present their passage as part of a local news show and read the reports as if being reported by Headline News. Assign the following passages: Acts 2:1-13,42-46; Acts 4:31-35; 1 Corinthians 11:17-34; 1 Corinthians 14:26-28; Ephesians 5:18-20; Colossians 3:15-17.

Section Two: God's Person (15 Minutes)

Paul: Missionary to the Gentiles

- Read Acts 7:57—8:3; 9:1-19 to the group.
- Invite volunteers from the group to share their conversion experiences. Especially encourage those who did not grow up in a Christian family or those who greatly disliked Christians or churches to share their conversion experiences. Saul's conversion led him to travel great distances to share the gospel of Christ. Discuss:

  What are some ways we can share the gospel today?

Make a list on the board as the group shares.

What kinds of persecution and difficulties do Christians face today in sharing the gospel?

Option Two: (For a 90-Minute Session)

Paul: Writer of Epistles (15 Minutes)

- Ask everyone to write a letter to someone—real or imagined—in a distant city. The letter should encourage the recipient to follow Jesus and live a holy life. Also send personal greetings to individual family members.
- Ask various volunteers to share the letters they have written. Then ask the group members to identify the main element in all of the letters. Write their input on the board.
- As an example, have everyone turn to 2 Thessalonians. Have the group identify the opening greeting and introduction, the main body of the letter and the closing comments and benediction. Your findings should be: Greeting and prayer: vv. 1:1-12; main body of the Epistle: vv. 2—3:15; final comments, personal greetings and benediction: vv. 3:16-18.

Section Three: God's Son (15 Minutes)

Jesus Christ Revealed as Lord of the Church

- Divide the whole group into four small groups. Give each group a sheet of newsprint and felt-tip pens. Ask each group to list how Christ is the Head of the Church and is leading according to their assigned passage. Ask them to also list how they see Jesus leading the local church in light

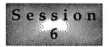

GOD'S STORY IN ACTS THROUGH PHILIPPIANS

1. Jesus sent the Holy Spirit to empower the Early Church to become His witnesses in Jerusalem, Judea, Samaria and the whole earth (see Acts 1:8).

   Notes:

2. God converted the Jewish persecutor of the early Church—Saul—into the missionary Paul to take the gospel message to the Gentiles throughout the Mediterranean world.

   Notes:

3. Paul wrote letters to churches throughout the known world to address problems and conflicts, to teach truth, combat heresy and encourage the new converts to Christianity.

   Notes:

4. After Paul's release from prison in A.D. 62-63, he traveled on his fourth missionary journey and wrote the "pastoral epistles" of 1 and 2 Timothy and Titus.

   Notes:

5. Paul's letters are filled with many teachings and exhortations.

   Notes:

CONTINUED

Before next session, read:
Sunday: First Church in Jerusalem (Acts 1:1—4:37)
Monday: Witnessing in Jerusalem (Acts 5:1—8:3)
Tuesday: Witnessing in Judea and Samaria (Acts 8:4—12:25)
Wednesday: Paul Establishes the Churches (First Tour) (Acts 13:1—15:35)
Thursday: Paul Revisits the Churches (Second Tour) (Acts 15:36—18:21)
Friday: Paul Encourages the Churches (Third Tour) (Acts 18:22—25:9)
Saturday: Paul Sent to Rome (Acts 25:10—28:31)

Understanding Acts

The purpose of this session is:

- To provide an overview of the book of Acts;
- To discover how Jesus Christ is revealed in Acts as the living Lord.

In this session, group members will learn:

- Key truths about God's story in Acts;
- That Jesus is revealed as the living Lord;
- The basic principle that the power of the Holy Spirit was demonstrated in many miracles and in the rapid growth of the Early Church;
- How to apply the truths revealed in Acts to their daily lives.

KEY VERSES

"'But you will receive power when the Holy Spirit comes on you; and you will be my witnesses in Jerusalem, and in all Judea and Samaria, and to the ends of the earth.'" Acts 1:8

"'Repent and be baptized, every one of you, in the name of Jesus Christ for the forgiveness of your sins. And you will receive the gift of the Holy Spirit. The promise is for you and your children and for all who are far off—for all whom the Lord our God will call.'" Acts 2:38

"All the believers were one in heart and mind. No one claimed that any of his possessions was his own, but they shared everything they had. With great power the apostles continued to testify to the resurrection of the Lord Jesus, and much grace was upon them all." Acts 4:32,33

BEFORE THE SESSION

- Pray for group members by name, asking the Holy Spirit to reveal to them the spiritual truths in Acts.
- Read chapter 32 of *What the Bible Is All About*.
- Prepare copies of Session 7 handouts "God's Story in Acts" and "Missionary Journeys of Paul" map for group members.
- Check off these supplies once you have secured them:
  - _____ A chalkboard and chalk or flip chart or overhead projector with markers.
  - _____ Extra Bibles, pencils and paper for group members.

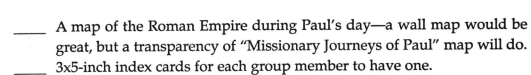

_____ A map of the Roman Empire during Paul's day—a wall map would be great, but a transparency of "Missionary Journeys of Paul" map will do.

_____ 3x5-inch index cards for each group member to have one.

- If you are having a 90-minute session, carefully read the two option sections right now and pull together any supplies you need for them.
- Read the entire session and look up every passage. Have your Bible *Tuck-In*™ page ready.
- Arrive early and be ready to warmly greet each group member as he or she arrives.
- Memorize the key verses. Share them periodically and ask the group to repeat them as you teach the session.

SECTION ONE: GOD'S STORY (20 MINUTES)

GOD'S STORY IN ACTS

Objective: To tell God's story so that Christians will apply the truths in the book of Acts to their own lives.

Greet everyone as they arrive. Tell the following story, doing the suggested activities as you come to them. Distribute the handouts "God's Story in Acts" and "Missionary Journeys of Paul" to all the group members.

Comparison of the Gospels and Acts

In this session, we move from Luke's Gospel proclamation about what Christ began on earth to what He continued to do through the power of His Holy Spirit in His Church in the book of Acts. Let's compare the Gospels and Acts (see Acts 1:1,2).

Read Acts 1:1,2 to the group. Put the following list on the board:

The Gospels present...	**Acts presents...**
The Son of Man coming to die for our sins.	The Son of God coming in the power of the Holy Spirit.
What Christ began to do.	What He continued to do through His Church by the Holy Spirit.

The crucified and risen Lord.	Christ as the ascended and exalted Lord.
The teachings of Christ.	The effects of His teachings on the apostles.
The calling and making of Jesus' disciples.	The empowering of His disciples to be His witnesses through the Holy Spirit.

Read Acts 1:8 and Matthew 28:19,20, then compare these two commands of Jesus. Discuss:

What are the marching orders of the Church?

How do we fulfill these commands today?

Where do we get the power to obey Christ's commission to us?

Holy Spirit Power for Witnessing (Acts 1—2)

God poured out His Holy Spirit at Pentecost giving the disciples and followers of Jesus the power and boldness to be His witnesses in Jerusalem (and throughout the known world) (see Acts 1:8; 2:1-21).

Read Acts 2:1-12. **At Babel in the Old Testament (see Genesis 11:1-9) God confused the languages of the world. How is Pentecost a reversal of Babel?** The Holy Spirit was poured out on one flesh and many different tongues could be understood to show that humanity could become one Body in Christ (cf. Galatians 3:26-29; Ephesians 2:11-22). Discuss:

Why was the ability to understand various languages important to the development of the Early Church?

Witnessing in Jerusalem (Acts 3:1—8:3)

Through signs and wonders, the Holy Spirit used the apostles to demonstrate the power and validity of the risen Lord. With unity through prayer, the apostles and the Early Church proclaimed the risen Jesus as Messiah and Lord with power and boldness (see Acts 4:31-33). After a time of phenomenal growth, severe persecution began to take place (see Acts 5:17,18,27,28, 33, 40; 6:8-15) and Stephen became the first martyr of the Church (see 7:54-60). Read Acts 8:1-3 and discuss: How did persecution help the Early Church to grow beyond Jerusalem?

Witnessing in Judea and Samaria (Acts 8:4—12:25)

From Jerusalem, Philip the evangelist took the gospel to Samaria and beyond (see Acts 8:1-8,26-40). The Jewish leader Saul, who persecuted, imprisoned and killed the Jewish believers in Jesus, met the risen Lord on the Damascus road. Saul—now the converted Paul—was called by God to become the apostle to the

Gentiles, traveling throughout the Roman Empire establishing churches (see Acts 8:1-3; 9:1-31).

Ask everyone to read Acts 8:26-40. Have everyone stand and push the chairs back so the room is cleared. Designate the wall on your right as "Difficult." Designate the wall on your left as "Easy." Ask group members to move to the wall that best answers each statement you read about witnessing. Then read the following situations and ask them to respond by moving to the area that best represents their answer. Ask one or two from each response area why they chose that answer.

Witnessing to an immediate family member.

Witnessing to a close family member like an aunt, uncle, cousin or niece.

Witnessing to a stranger.

Witnessing to an enemy.

Witnessing to a neighbor.

Witnessing to the Uttermost Parts of the Known World (Acts 13—28)

Paul's missionary journeys in Acts took the gospel to Asia Minor, Greece and finally Rome (see Acts 15:22-35; 17:1-33).

Before the first missionary journey, the Church overwhelmingly consisted of Jewish believers in Jesus. However, the success of the first journey made it apparent that the gospel was indeed Good News to the Gentiles as well. Now the Early Church had to face a potentially divisive issue head-on: Would non-Jewish believers be expected to keep the Mosaic Law (see Acts 15:1-5)? The Jerusalem Council made an unambiguous decision. They understood clearly that Jewish and Gentile believers were saved and that both had received the Holy Spirit in exactly the same way—not by keeping the Mosaic Law but by faith in Jesus Christ. Therefore, the Council decided that Jews should not put cultural roadblocks in the way of Gentiles who were turning to God and that new Gentile believers should avoid offending religious Jews who wanted to believe in Jesus but also continue their traditions (see Acts 15:8-21).

Discuss:

What was the result of this decision? (It enabled the Early Church to expand from being a minority Jewish sect to a dynamic, multicultural missionary movement that spread the gospel throughout the world.)

Discuss ways in which our Christian cultural way of doing things may hinder people who may be seeking a relationship with God. **How can our church become more of a missionary church?**

OPTION ONE: (FOR A 90-MINUTE SESSION)

Be My Witnesses (15 Minutes)

Have the group form pairs and turn to the handout section entitled "Be My Witnesses."

In Acts, the word witness, *martus,* is used over thirty times. Let's explore what a witness is and does.

Ask the pairs to work as a team and look up the Scriptures and help one another discover how the Early Church witnessed for Jesus Christ. After the pairs have completed their Scripture discoveries, discuss the following with the whole group:

In what ways did God use the Early Church to witness?

How does the Holy Spirit demonstrate His power in us as witnesses today?

What would increase our boldness as witnesses?

SECTION TWO: GOD'S PERSON (15 MINUTES)

BARNABAS: SON OF ENCOURAGEMENT

Objective: To discover how an early follower of Jesus was used by the Holy Spirit in a powerful way just as we can be.

A Jewish believer from Cyprus named Joseph was given the name Barnabas by the apostles because he was so encouraging. In fact, the name Barnabas is derived from one of the titles of the Holy Spirit: *paraclete:* encourager, one who stands beside.

Divide the group into four groups. Assign each group one of the following chapters: Acts 11:19-30; 13:1-14,42-52; 14:1-7,12-28; 15:1-14,35-41. Instruct the small groups to read their assigned verses and summarize Barnabas's ministry. After about seven minutes, have the small groups report to the whole group. List on the board, flip chart or overhead all the qualities that Barnabas had as an encourager and witness for Jesus Christ. Save this list to be used during the "Pursuing God" activity.

OPTION TWO: (FOR A 90-MINUTE SESSION)

Three Witnessing Journeys (15 Minutes)

Divide the group into three small groups and assign each group one of Paul's missionary journeys. Using the map handout "Missionary Journeys of Paul," find all the places Paul went to establish churches.

Journey One: Acts 13:4—14:28
Journey Two: Acts 15:39—18:22
Journey Three: Acts 27:1—28:16

Have each group trace Paul's journeys on one of their map handouts and if possible transferred to a wall map or a transparency of the handout. After all the journeys have been reported and tracked on the larger map, discuss:

What trials and difficulties did Paul face?

How is being a missionary different today?

How can we be involved in missionary work?

How is our church reaching out to the world with the gospel?

SECTION THREE: GOD'S SON (15 MINUTES)

JESUS CHRIST REVEALED AS THE LIVING LORD

Objective: To see how Jesus is revealed in Acts as the living Lord.

The power of the risen, living Lord is demonstrated through signs and wonders in the book of Acts. Assign various group members to read the following verses: Acts 2:1-13; Acts 2:42-47; Acts 3:1-10; Acts 4:23-31; Acts 5:12-16; Acts 9:1-19.

List the different ways the living Lord manifested His power after each passage is read. Circle those ways in which they have also seen His power manifested today. Invite any group members who wish to share one way they have witnessed the power of the living Lord in their personal lives.

PURSUING GOD (5 MINUTES)

NEXT STEPS I NEED TO TAKE

Objective: To take a realistic assessment of one's relationship with Jesus and how that relationship might grow closer in the coming week.

Read the previously listed qualities in Barnabas's life. Form pairs and ask the partners to share their completions of the following statements which you have written on the board, flip chart or overhead:

One quality that needs to grow in my life is...

One quality that God is really using in my life right now is...

PRAYER (5 MINUTES)

Objective: To pray in one accord like the Early Church prayed.

Read Acts 4:24-30. Give each group member a 3x5-inch index card. Ask everyone to write down a prayer concern that focuses on each of the following issues:

Families;

The local church;

Governmental leaders;

The Church around the world;

The poor;

The sick.

Read each topic and have group members share what they have written down. When certain concerns are mentioned over and over again, circle them. For those concerns that the Holy Spirit seems to be putting on many hearts, ask various group members to pray for those specific concerns, representing the unity and agreement of corporate prayer.

Session 7 Bible *Tuck-In*™

UNDERSTANDING ACTS

The purpose of this session is:

- To provide an overview of book of Acts;
- To discover how Jesus Christ is revealed in Acts as the living Lord.

KEY VERSES

"But you will receive power when the Holy Spirit comes on you; and you will be my witnesses in Jerusalem, and in all Judea and Samaria, and to the ends of the earth.'" Acts 1:8

"Repent and be baptized, every one of you, in the name of Jesus Christ for the forgiveness of your sins. And you will receive the gift of the Holy Spirit. The promise is for you and your children and for all who are far off—for all whom the Lord our God will call.'" Acts 2:38

"All the believers were one in heart and mind. No one claimed that any of his possessions was his own, but they shared everything they had. With great power the apostles continued to testify to the resurrection of the Lord Jesus, and much grace was upon them all." Acts 4:32,33

---

which they have seen His power manifested today. Invite any group members who wish to share one way they have witnessed the power of the living Lord in their personal lives.

PURSUING GOD (5 MINUTES)

NEXT STEPS I NEED TO TAKE

- Read the previously listed qualities of Barnabas's life. Form pairs and ask each partner to share his or her completion to the following statements which you have written on the board, flip chart or overhead:

  One quality that needs to grow in my life is...

  One quality that God really uses now in my life is...

PRAYER (5 MINUTES)

- Read Acts 4:24-30. Give each group member a 3x5-inch index card. Ask everyone to write down a prayer concern that focuses on each of the following issues:

  Families;
  The local church;
  Governmental leaders;
  The Church around the world;
  The poor;
  The sick.

- Read each topic and have group members share what they have written down. When certain concerns are mentioned over and over again, circle them. For those concerns that the Holy Spirit seems to be putting on many hearts, ask various group members to pray for those specific concerns, representing the unity and agreement of corporate prayer.

SECTION ONE: GOD'S STORY (20 MINUTES)

GOD'S STORY IN ACTS

- Greet everyone as they arrive. Tell the story of the book of Acts, doing the suggested activities as you come to them. Distribute the handout "God's Story in Acts" to group members.

OPTION ONE: (FOR A 90-MINUTE SESSION)

Be My Witnesses (15 Minutes)

- Have the group members form pairs and turn to the hand-out section entitled "Be My Witnesses."
- Ask the pairs to work together to look up the Scriptures and help one another discover how the Early Church witnessed for Jesus Christ. After the pairs have completed their Scripture discoveries, discuss the following with the whole group:

  In what ways did God use the Early Church to witness?

  How does the Holy Spirit demonstrate His power in us as witnesses today?

  What would increase our boldness as witnesses?

SECTION TWO: GOD'S PERSON (15 MINUTES)

BARNABAS: SON OF ENCOURAGEMENT

- Divide the group into four groups. Assign each group one of the following chapters: Acts 11:19-30; 13:1-14,42-52; 14:1-7,12-28; 15:1-14,35-41. Instruct the small groups to read their assigned verses and summarize Barnabas's ministry.
- After about seven minutes, have the small groups report to the whole group. List on the board, flip chart or overhead

--- Fold ---

all the qualities that Barnabas had as an encourager and witness for Jesus Christ. Save this list to be used during the "Pursuing God" activity.

OPTION TWO: (FOR A 90-MINUTE SESSION)

Three Witnessing Journeys (15 Minutes)

- Using a map of the Roman Empire in Paul's day, find all the places Paul went to establish churches. Divide the group into three small groups and assign each group one of Paul's missionary journeys.

Journey One:	Acts 13:4—14:28
Journey Two:	Acts 15:39—8:22
Journey Three:	Acts 27:1—28:16

- Have each group trace Paul's journeys on one of their maps or on a big map and then report to the whole group. After all the journeys have been reported, discuss:

  What trials and difficulties did Paul face?

  How is being a missionary different today?

  How can we be involved in missionary work?

  How is our church reaching out to the world with the gospel?

SECTION THREE: GOD'S SON (15 MINUTES)

JESUS CHRIST REVEALED AS THE LIVING LORD

- The power of the risen, living Lord is demonstrated through signs and wonders in the book of Acts. Assign various group members to read: Acts 2:1-13; Acts 2:42-47; Acts 3:1-10; Acts 4:23-31; Acts 5:12-16; Acts 9:1-19.
- List the different ways the living Lord manifested His power after each passage is read. Circle those ways in

GOD'S STORY IN ACTS

1. Comparison of the Gospels and Acts

    Notes:

2. Holy Spirit Power for Witnessing (Acts 1—2)

    Notes:

3. Witnessing in Jerusalem (Acts 3:1—8:3)

    Notes:

4. Witnessing in Judea and Samaria (Acts 8:4—12:25)

    Notes:

5. Witnessing to the Uttermost Parts of the Known World (Acts 13—28)

    Notes:

BE MY WITNESSES

What does Acts say about being a witness for Christ?

Acts 1:8 _____

Acts 4:29-33 _____

Acts 5:32 _____

Acts 10:39-41 _____

Acts 22:14-16 _____

Before next session, read:

Sunday: What We Are by Nature (Romans 1:1—3:20)

Monday: How to Become a Christian (Romans 3:21—5:21)

Tuesday: How to Live the Christian Life (Romans 6:1-23)

Wednesday: A Struggle (Romans 7:1-25)

Thursday: The Life of Victory (Romans 8:1-39)

Friday: The Jews Set Aside (Romans 9:30—11:12)

Saturday: The Christian's Service (Romans 12:1-21)

MISSIONARY JOURNEYS OF PAUL

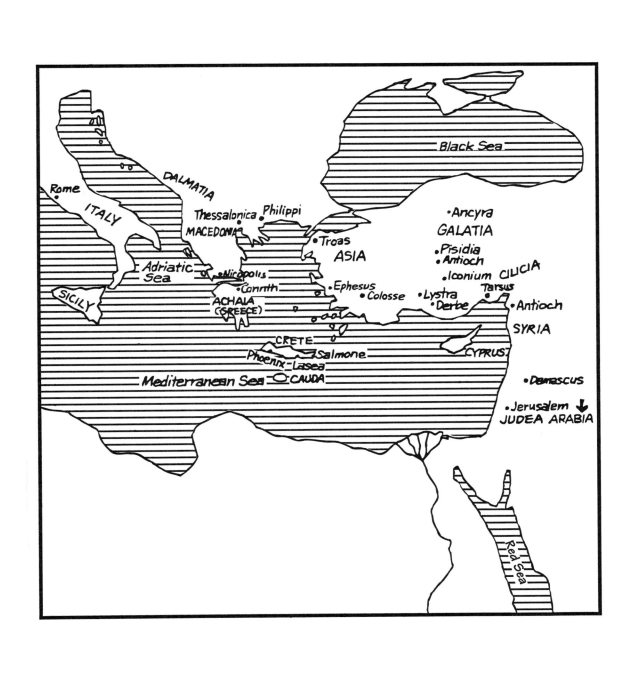

Understanding Romans

The purpose of this session is:
- To provide an overview of Paul's Epistle to the Romans;
- To discover how Jesus Christ is revealed in Romans as our Righteousness.

In this session, group members will learn:
- Key truths about God's story in Romans;
- How Jesus is revealed as our Righteousness;
- The basic principle that there is no righteousness apart from Jesus Christ because all have sinned and departed from God's law and righteousness;
- How to apply the truths revealed in Romans to their daily lives.

KEY VERSES

"I am not ashamed of the gospel, because it is the power of God for the salvation of everyone who believes: first for the Jew, then for the Gentile. For in the gospel a righteousness from God is revealed, a righteousness that is by faith from first to last, just as it is written: 'The righteous will live by faith.'" Romans 1:16,17

"This righteousness from God comes through faith in Jesus Christ to all who believe. There is no difference, for all have sinned and fall short of the glory of God, and are justified freely by his grace through the redemption that came by Christ Jesus." Romans 3:22-24

"Therefore, since we have been justified through faith, we have peace with God through our Lord Jesus Christ, through whom we have gained access by faith into this grace in which we now stand." Romans 5:1,2

"That if you confess with your mouth, 'Jesus is Lord,' and believe in your heart that God raised him from the dead, you will be saved." Romans 10:9

BEFORE THE SESSION

- Pray for group members by name, asking the Holy Spirit to reveal to them the spiritual truths in Romans.
- Read Chapter 33 in *What the Bible Is All About.*
- Prepare copies of Session 8 handout "God's Story in Romans" for all group members.
- Check off these supplies once you have secured them:

    ____ A chalkboard and chalk or flip chart or overhead projector with markers.

    ____ Extra Bibles, pencils and paper for group members.

    ____ Newsprint, felt-tip pen and masking tape.

    ____ A wastepaper basket and paper for everyone in the group.

- If you are having a 90-minute session, carefully read the two option sections right now and pull together any supplies you need for them.
- Read the entire session and look up every passage. Have your Bible *Tuck-In*™ page ready.
- Arrive early and be ready to warmly greet each group member as he or she arrives.
- Memorize the key verses. Share them periodically and ask the group to repeat them as you teach the session.

SECTION ONE: GOD'S STORY (20 MINUTES)

GOD'S STORY IN ROMANS

Objective: To tell God's story so that Christians will apply the truths in Romans in their own lives.

    Greet everyone as they arrive. Tell the following story, doing the suggested activities as you come to them. Distribute the handout "God's Story in Romans" to group members.

Paul the Apostle (Romans 1:1-17)

We now begin a study of the Epistles in the New Testament. Since you are now beginning the letters of the New Testament, it is appropriate to pause and give a brief overview of Paul who penned the majority of the epistles. Thirteen of the twenty-one letters were written by Paul; these are called the Pauline Epistles. He wrote his letters to the churches at Thessalonica, Galatia, Corinth and Rome during his missionary journeys. While he was a prisoner in Rome, he wrote his letters to the Ephesians, the Colossians, Philemon and the Philippians. After his imprisonment he wrote two letters to Timothy and one to Titus.

    Paul was born at Tarsus, of pure Jewish stock. His teacher was Gamaliel, the great teacher of the Pharisees. Like all Hebrew boys, he learned a trade—he was a tentmaker. In Jerusalem he was present at the stoning of Stephen, the first

Christian martyr (see Acts 7:54—8:3). On the way to Damascus on his mission to persecute the Christians, the young Pharisee had a head-on collision with Jesus Christ (see Acts 9:1-19)! After his miraculous conversion, he was baptized and received his commission to preach the gospel. He retired to Arabia and spent three years there in study and preparation.

After laboring for three years in Tarsus and one year in Antioch, Paul was directed by the Holy Spirit to become the first missionary to the Gentiles. On his three missionary journeys he founded many churches and wrote his Epistles. The combination of Roman citizenship, Greek education and Hebrew religion wonderfully qualified him for his great work, but you will find that he trusted alone in the grace and apostleship which he received directly from Jesus Christ (see Romans 1:5).

After a life filled with sacrifice and suffering, he sealed his testimony with his own life's blood. Tradition says he was beheaded at Rome, and his body buried in the catacombs (adapted from *What the Bible Is All About*, pp. 431-432).

Have group members read Romans 1:1-17 and add any details that they find about Paul's life to what you have already listed on the board.

The Church at Rome (Romans 1:1-16)

Eager to visit the church in Rome, Paul sent them this letter from Corinth while he was on his third missionary journey.

Written in about the fourth year of Nero's reign, Paul uses this letter to summarize and plumb the depths of the gospel of Jesus Christ.

Read Romans 1:16,17, then discuss:

What makes Christians ashamed of the gospel?

What is the fear that keeps us from sharing the gospel—fear of rejection, fear of the unknown, fear of involvement? Why?

What We Are by Nature (Romans 1:1—3:20)

Humanity in its sinful state turns away from God and worships the creature instead of the Creator. Both Jew and Gentile alike are guilty before God. Though the Jew has God's law, he rebels. Though the Gentile has God's revelation in creation, he rebels. All are under sin (see Romans 3:9-30).

Discuss:

How is God revealed in creation?

Why do people seem to naturally rebel against any law?

Even young children have the natural inclination to disobey. Share examples of how your young children willfully disobeyed you.

How to Become a Christian (Romans 3:21—5:21)

When Christ's righteousness is given to us, this is called justification which means to be made just (righteous) before God. In Romans we learn that God saves sinners by faith, that is, they trust in Jesus Christ as their righteousness (see Romans 3:21-26; 5:1,2).

Ask each person to complete the section in their handout entitled "How To Become a Christian." Then discuss the following with the whole group:

How are we justified before God?

What do we receive by faith?

What is the purpose of good works?

Take a moment to lead the group in the sinner's prayer. For those who are saved, this will be a moment of thanksgiving and rejoicing in what God has done in their lives. For those who are seeking, this will be a time of giving their lives to Jesus Christ.

> **Heavenly Father, based on Romans 3:23, I confess that I am a sinner and repent of my sin. Claiming Romans 3:24,25, I receive Jesus' redemption from sin by His shed blood. Responding to Romans 10:9, I confess with my mouth that Jesus is the Christ, the Son of the living God, my Lord and Savior, and I believe in my heart that God raised Jesus from the dead. I receive the gift of the Holy Spirit and eternal life in Jesus' name. Amen.**

How to Live the Christian Life (Romans 6—8)

When we were baptized into Christ, our old lives, which were lived according to our sinful natures, died (see Romans 6:1-14). **As believers, we now have new lives that we live according to the Spirit, who controls us, has adopted us and prays through us** (see 6:9-11; 8:26,27).

Have group members share some struggles that they personally have in trying to live a holy and righteous life.

Say: **In our own strength, it's impossible to live the Christian life. Paul writes about that struggle.** Read Romans 7:15-25.

Divide the group into groups of three or four. Ask each person to share his or her completion of the following statements with their small groups:

The hardest struggle I have in dying to self is ...

The Spirit has helped me to ...

Israel's Response to Christ (Romans 9—11)

Paul explained that Israel's rejection of Jesus as the promised Messiah (see Romans 10:16) **opened the way for the Gentiles to be grafted into God's people** (see 11:11-24). **Paul still hoped for and praised God for the day when Israel would acknowledge Jesus as Lord** (see 11:25-36).

With the whole group, review what you remember from the Old Testament about Israel's repeated rejection of God and disobedience of His commands. **Although a minority of the Jews accepted Jesus as the promised Messiah, Israel as a whole rejected Him. As a result, Israel has been set aside and scattered among the nations.** Discuss:

How do you see God working today for the salvation of Israel through establishing both the nation of Israel and raising up messianic Jews—Jewish believers in Jesus as Messiah—around the world?

How to Serve God (Romans 12—16)

Serving God springs out of our love for Him and is translated into our love and service to others (see 12:9,10; 13:8-10; 15:1-7). As we live according to the Spirit, we will abstain from evil and perform good deeds that bless the lives of others (see 12:9-21; 13:8-14).

Ask group members to return to their groups of three or four and to first of all fill out the checklist under section 7 on their handouts and then to share with each other one thing that they learned about themselves from filling out their checklists.

OPTION ONE: (FOR A 90-MINUTE SESSION)

Living According to the Spirit (15 Minutes)

Romans 8 is one of the greatest chapters in the Bible because it teaches us how to live as Christians. Let's explore it together.

Divide the verses equally among the group members. (For example, there are 39 verses in the chapter; so if there are ten people in your group, assign each person about four verses each.) Ask everyone to read their assigned verses and to summarize their assigned verse(s) in one sentence. Have everyone write their sentences on the sheets of newsprint or poster board that you have previously taped to the walls around the room. Then have everyone walk around and read the summaries. Discuss:

How can we get ourselves out of the way so that the Spirit can have control in our lives?

Section Two: God's Person (15 Minutes)

The Person of Faith

Objective: To discover how we can live by faith and walk in God's Spirit.

Divide the group into pairs. Give the following instructions: **The shortest one in each pair will be the leader and the tallest will be the one led. The one being led needs to shut his or her eyes and cover them with both hands. For one minute, the leader will give verbal directions for the person with his or her eyes closed to walk around the room without bumping into anything or anyone. After a minute, I will say "Touch" and then the leader will lead the follower around the room by the elbow. After the second minute, we will switch and have the follower become the leader and the leader the follower. We will then repeat the activity.**

After the pairs have done this "faith" activity, discuss with the whole group: **Which is harder—trusting someone giving verbal instructions or someone leading you by touch? Explain.**
What feelings did you have as you were being led around?
How is this like trusting Jesus to lead you by His Spirit?

Have everyone read Romans 5:1-5. **Faith is trusting the Holy Spirit's leading even when we cannot fully understand what He is doing at the moment. As we trust Him, He builds hope in us through suffering and perseverance which produce character.**

Have group members find their previous partners. Have them share what is most difficult for them to trust God for. Ask them to share what God is doing right now in their lives to produce character and faith.

Option Two: (For a 90-Minute Session)

Law vs. Grace (15 Minutes)

Read Romans 7:14-25 to the group. **At times in his life, Paul failed to meet his own expectations and God's in spite of his best efforts. How have we experienced**

what Paul is talking about here in Romans 7? Ask for three or four volunteers to share a time when they were determined to do right but still ended up doing something wrong, or to share a time when they worked hard to be perfect but still fell short of their or others' expectations.

Have group members return to their partners. Write the following words across the board, flip chart or overhead:

Guilty   Frustrated   Disappointed   Dumb   Angry   Numb

Ask the pairs to share with each other their feelings when they encounter each of the following situations. Read the first situation and then give the pairs time to share their feelings before moving on to the next situation. **How do you feel when you...**

1. **Fail a test?**
2. **Forget a birthday or anniversary?**
3. **Completely forget an appointment or meeting?**
4. **Start a project but are unable to finish it?**
5. **Apply for a job, but don't get it?**
6. **Apply for a desperately needed loan and get turned down?**
7. **Find yourself breaking one of God's commandments and not even trying to do what's right?**

Discuss the following with the whole group:

What should we do if we feel guilty about not meeting our own expectations or those of others?

What should we do if our guilt comes from falling short of God's righteousness? When God in His grace—a gift from God—forgives us, why shouldn't we feel free to keep on sinning since we know we will be forgiven? Refer to Romans 6:1-4 in this discussion.

SECTION THREE: GOD'S SON (15 MINUTES)

JESUS CHRIST REVEALED AS OUR RIGHTEOUSNESS

Objective: To see how Jesus is revealed in Romans as our Righteousness.

Read Isaiah 64:6 and Romans 3:23. With the group, list the things that do not make us righteous in the eyes of God. Write what they share on the board, flip chart or overhead.

Righteousness—*dikaiosune*—means to fulfill God's law, to be blameless, to

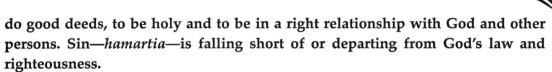

do good deeds, to be holy and to be in a right relationship with God and other persons. Sin—*hamartia*—is falling short of or departing from God's law and righteousness.

Give everyone paper to crumple up into a ball. Have a wastepaper basket in the front of the room. Ask everyone to try to throw their paper balls into the basket. Most will miss. A few may hit the basket. Ask those who make a basket to throw another one into the basket from where they are. Discuss:

Is it possible to make a basket 100 percent of the time?

Sin means missing the mark. Why is it impossible for humans to be righteous apart from Jesus Christ?

Now ask for one volunteer. Give that person about five paper balls. Have him or her throw you the paper balls one at a time. You pick them up and put all of them in the basket. As you are doing this, say: **Jesus takes our unrighteousness and becomes righteousness for us.**

Have everyone read Romans 4:4,5 in unison.

PURSUING GOD (5 MINUTES)

NEXT STEPS I NEED TO TAKE

Objective: To take a realistic assessment of one's relationship with Jesus and how that relationship might grow closer in the coming week.

Have everyone turn to the handout and fill out the section labeled "Righteous Living." Once each person has completed this, divide into pairs and ask the pairs to share how they have filled out this section.

PRAYER (5 MINUTES)

Objective: To pray Paul's prayer in our own lives from Romans 16:25-27.

Ask each person to read Romans 16:25-27 silently. Now have the partners pray this prayer out loud for each other. Have the whole group form a circle. As the leader, read Romans 16:25-27 a phrase at a time and have them repeat each phrase out loud after you.

Session 8 Bible *Tuck-In*™

UNDERSTANDING ROMANS

The purpose of this session is:

- To provide an overview of Paul's Epistle to the Romans;
- To discover how Jesus Christ is revealed in Romans as our Righteousness.

KEY VERSES

"I am not ashamed of the gospel, because it is the power of God for the salvation of everyone who believes: first for the Jew, then for the Gentile. For in the gospel a righteousness from God is revealed, a righteousness that is by faith from first to last, just as it is written: 'The righteous will live by faith.'" Romans 1:16,17

"This righteousness from God comes through faith in Jesus Christ to all who believe. There is no difference, for all have sinned and fall short of the glory of God, and are justified freely by his grace through the redemption that came by Christ Jesus." Romans 3:22-24

"Therefore, since we have been justified through faith, we have peace with God through our Lord Jesus Christ, through whom we have gained access by faith into this grace in which we now stand." Romans 5:1,2

SECTION THREE: GOD'S SON (15 MINUTES)

JESUS CHRIST REVEALED AS OUR RIGHTEOUSNESS

- Read Isaiah 64:6 and Romans 3:23. List the things that do not make us righteous in the eyes of God.

- Explain righteousness to the group. Give everyone paper to crumple up into a ball. Have a wastepaper basket in the front of the room. Ask everyone to try to throw their paper balls into the basket. Ask those who make a basket to throw another one into the basket from where they are. Discuss: **Is it possible to make a basket 100 percent of the time? Why is it impossible for humans to be righteous apart from Jesus Christ?** Sin means missing the mark.

- Now ask for one volunteer. Have him or her throw you five paper balls one at a time. Pick them up and put all of them in the basket. As you are doing this, say: **Jesus takes our unrighteousness and becomes righteousness for us.** Read Romans 4:4,5 in unison.

PURSUING GOD (5 MINUTES)

NEXT STEPS I NEED TO TAKE

- Have everyone turn to the handout and fill out the section labeled "Righteous Living." Divide into pairs and ask them to share how they have filled out this section.

PRAYER (5 MINUTES)

- Ask each person to read Romans 16:25-27 silently. Now have the partners pray this prayer out loud for each other. Have the whole group form a circle. As the leader, read Romans 16:25-27 a phrase at a time and have them repeat each phrase out loud after you.

"That if you confess with your mouth, 'Jesus is Lord,' and believe in your heart that God raised him from the dead, you will be saved." Romans 10:9

SECTION ONE: GOD'S STORY (20 MINUTES)

GOD'S STORY IN ROMANS
- Greet everyone as they arrive. Tell the story, doing the suggested activities as you come to them. Distribute the hand-out "God's Story in Romans" to group members.

OPTION ONE: (FOR A 90-MINUTE SESSION)

Living According to the Spirit (15 Minutes)
- Divide the verses equally among the group members. Ask everyone to read their assigned verses and to summarize their verse(s) in one sentence. Have everyone write their sentences on the newsprint or poster board. Then have everyone walk around and read the summaries. Discuss: How can we get ourselves out of the way so that the Spirit can have control in our lives?

SECTION TWO: GOD'S PERSON (15 MINUTES)

THE PERSON OF FAITH
- Divide the group into pairs. Give the instructions for the faith walk. After the pairs have done this "faith" activity, discuss with the whole group:
Which is harder: trusting someone giving verbal instructions or someone leading you by touch? Explain. What feelings did you have as you were being led around? How is this like trusting Jesus to lead you by His Spirit?

- Read Romans 5:1-5, then have them find partners and share what's most difficult for them to trust God for and what God is doing right now in their lives to produce character and faith.

OPTION TWO: (FOR A 90-MINUTE SESSION)

Law vs. Grace (15 Minutes)
- Read Romans 7:14-25. Ask for three or four volunteers to share a time when they were determined to do right but still ended up doing something wrong, or a time when they worked hard to be perfect but still fell short of their or others' expectations. Have them return to their partners. Write the following words on the board:
Guilty   Frustrated   Disappointed   Dumb   Angry   Numb
- Ask the pairs to share their feelings when they encounter each of the following situations. Read the first situation and give the pairs time to share feelings before moving on to the next situation. How do you feel when you: (1) Fail a test? (2) Forget a birthday or anniversary? (3) Completely forget an appointment or meeting? (4) Start a project but are unable to finish it? (5) Apply for a job but don't get it? (6) Apply for a desperately needed loan and get turned down? (7) Find yourself breaking one of God's commandments and not even trying to do what's right?
- With the whole group, discuss:
What should we do if we feel guilty about not meeting our own expectations or those of others? What should we do if our guilt comes from falling short of God's righteousness? When God in His grace—a gift—forgives us, why shouldn't we feel free to keep on sinning since we know we will be forgiven? Refer to Romans 6:1-4 in this discussion.

GOD'S STORY IN ROMANS

1. Paul the Apostle (Romans 1:1-17)

   Notes:

2. The Church at Rome (Romans 1:1-16)

   Notes:

3. What We Are by Nature (Romans 1:1—3:20)

   Notes:

4. How to Become a Christian (Romans 3:21—5:21)

   a. Justification means to…

   b. Faith means to…

CONTINUED

c. Who is righteous or good apart from God (see Romans 3:23)?

d. What does God see when He looks at us outside apart from Christ (see Romans 3:10)?

e. We, like Abraham, receive what three things by faith (see Romans 4:3,13,17)?

God imparts or grants righteousness to us by grace (see Romans 3:24); Jesus' shed blood (vv. 24,25); and our faith (v. 22), producing in us the experience of God's blessing (Romans 5:1-4) and good works (Romans 12:9-21). Write a sentence prayer thanking God for justifying you by faith in Jesus Christ.

5. How to Live the Christian Life (Romans 6—8)

    Notes:

6. Israel's Response to Christ (Romans 9—11)

    Notes:

CONTINUED

7. How to Serve God (Romans 12—16)

   Paul gives us a checklist for living according to the Spirit, not according to the flesh. This checklist is based on Romans 12—13. Put yourself on the line with a check mark.

Righteous Living

a.	Love sincerely.	Never	Always
b.	Hate evil.	Never	Always
c.	Honor others above myself.	Never	Always
d.	Enthusiastically serve God.	Never	Always
e.	Joyful in hope.	Never	Always
f.	Patient in affliction.	Never	Always
g.	Faithful in prayer.	Never	Always
h.	Share with the needy.	Never	Always
i.	Practice hospitality.	Never	Always
j.	Not conceited.	Never	Always
k.	Overcome evil with good.	Never	Always
l.	Owe no one anything but love.	Never	Always
m.	Put aside the deeds of darkness.	Never	Always

CONTINUED

n. Do not think about satisfying my desires.   <u>Never</u>   <u>Always</u>

o. Clothe myself with Jesus Christ.   <u>Never</u>   <u>Always</u>

Before the next session, read:
Sunday: Division in the Church (1 Corinthians 1:10-31)
Monday: Human Wisdom (1 Corinthians 2:1-16)
Tuesday: Worldliness in the Church (1 Corinthians 3:1-23)
Wednesday: Immorality in the Church (1 Corinthians 5:1-13)
Thursday: The Lord's Supper (1 Corinthians 11:1-34)
Friday: Hymn of Love (1 Corinthians 13:1-13)
Saturday: The Resurrection (1 Corinthians 15:1-58)

Understanding 1 Corinthians

The purpose of this session is:

*   To provide an overview of Paul's first Epistle to the Corinthians;
*   To discover how Jesus Christ is revealed in 1 Corinthians as our Lord.

In this session, group members will learn:

*   Key truths about God's story in 1 Corinthians;
*   That Jesus is revealed as our Lord;
*   The basic principles that believers are to live in unity and moral purity, using their spiritual gifts to minister to one another in godly love;
*   How to apply the truths revealed in 1 Corinthians to their daily lives.

KEY VERSES

"For the message of the cross is foolishness to those who are perishing, but to us who are being saved it is the power of God." 1 Corinthians 1:18

"Don't you know that you yourselves are God's temple and that God's Spirit lives in you?" 1 Corinthians 3:16

"The Lord Jesus, on the night he was betrayed, took bread, and when he had given thanks, he broke it and said, 'This is my body, which is for you; do this in remembrance of me.' In the same way, after supper he took the cup, saying, 'This cup is the new covenant in my blood; do this, whenever you drink it, in remembrance of me.'" 1 Corinthians 11:23-25

"There are different kinds of gifts, but the same Spirit. There are different kinds of service, but the same Lord. There are different kinds of working, but the same God works all of them in all men." 1 Corinthians 12:4-6

"If I speak in the tongues of men and of angels, but have not love, I am only a resounding gong or a clanging cymbal." 1 Corinthians 13:1

"And if Christ has not been raised, our preaching is useless and so is your faith." 1 Corinthians 15:14

BEFORE THE SESSION

- Pray for group members by name, asking the Holy Spirit to reveal to them the spiritual truths in 1 Corinthians.
- Read chapter 34 in *What the Bible Is All About*.
- Prepare copies of Session 9 handout "God's Story in 1 Corinthians" for all group members.
- Check off these supplies once you have secured them:
  - ____ A chalkboard and chalk or flip chart or overhead projector with markers.
  - ____ Extra Bibles, pencils and paper for group members.
  - ____ If you plan to do Option One and celebrate the Lord's Supper, be certain to have the elements for communion and invite your pastor to share with you if it is appropriate.
- If you are having a 90-minute session, carefully read the two option sections right now and pull together any supplies you need for them.
- Read the entire session and look up every passage. Have your Bible *Tuck-In*™ page ready.
- Arrive early and be ready to warmly greet each group member as he or she arrives.
- Memorize the key verses. Share them periodically and ask the group to repeat them as you teach the session.

SECTION ONE: GOD'S STORY (20 MINUTES)

GOD'S STORY IN 1 CORINTHIANS

Objective: To tell God's story so that Christians will apply the truths in 1 Corinthians to their own lives.

Greet everyone as they arrive. Tell the following story, doing the suggested activities as you come to them. Distribute the handout "God's Story in 1 Corinthians" to all the group members.

The City of Corinth (1 Corinthians 1:2)

Corinth was the most important city in all of Greece during Paul's day. A wealthy trade center, Corinth's men spent their days in tournaments and speeches. Luxury, dissipation and public immorality were rampant in this great industrial, seafaring population. Corinth attracted great crowds of foreigners from the east and the west. Their gods were gods of pleasure and lust. Much emphasis was placed on culture and the arts. Corinth abounded in schools of language and philosophy. As in most cities, there was a large colony of Jews who had kept their strong moral standards and held to their Jewish beliefs. The city itself was the center of a debased form of the worship of Venus.

Have everyone read 1 Corinthians 1:1-17. List what they learn about the Corinthian church from these verses on the board, flip chart or overhead.

Corrections in Christian Conduct (1 Corinthians 1—11)

Instead of the church influencing the culture, the opposite was happening at Corinth. Worldliness, division and immorality were creeping into the church. Paul stressed the need for the wisdom of Christ (see 1 Corinthians 1:18—2:16); for unity in the church (see 3:1—4:20); for morality and pure living (see 5—10); and for propriety and dignity in worship (see chapter 11).

Divide the group into four groups. Assign one of the following titles and its accompanying verses to each group—Wisdom, Morality, Worship or Unity:

Wisdom Group:	1 Corinthians 1—2
Unity Group:	1 Corinthians 3—4
Morality Group:	1 Corinthians 6; 7:1-7; 10:14-22
Worship Group:	1 Corinthians 11

Instruct each small group to write a brief summary of Paul's teaching on their assigned topic and then share it with the whole group. After their summaries are given, discuss:

What counterfeits for God's wisdom does the world offer today?

What causes disunity in the Church today?

What evidences of immorality and compromise caused by the influence of the world do we see in today's Church?

According to Paul, how are we to respond to these issues?

Instructions for Christian Conduct (1 Corinthians 12—16)

Paul instructed believers on ministering to one another with our gifts of the Holy Spirit (see 1 Corinthians 12; 14); on showing godly love (*agape*) to one another (see 1 Corinthians 13); and on giving to help others (see 1 Corinthians 16).

Have the group form a tight circle with shoulders touching. Then have them all make one half turn to the right so they are facing the back of the person on their right. Give the following instructions: **On the count of three, everyone will carefully sit down on the lap of the person behind them. If we do this together, we will all work in unity and be able to support one another. If we are not together, we will all fall. Once we are seated, I will count to three and everyone will stand up together.**

After this exercise, read 1 Corinthians 12:12,26. Discuss:

What do these verses say about how we can support others in the Body of Christ?
After the discussion, have group members share with the whole group things that they are rejoicing over. Then have members share prayer concerns.

Pray for the needs of the local Body of Christ.

The Pillars of the Gospel (1 Corinthians 15)

Paul proclaimed to the Corinthians that the core of the gospel is the resurrection of Jesus. If Christ were not raised from the dead, there would be no gospel (see 15:1-19). Paul defined the pillars of the gospel as:

1. **Jesus' resurrection**
2. **His coming again**
3. **Believers will be raised**
4. **Christ will defeat His enemies**
5. **He will reign in glory**
6. **We will have immortality in eternal life**

Have group members share all the evidences of the resurrection of Jesus that they can remember. List these evidences on the board, flip chart or overhead. Read 1 Corinthians 15:1-19. List the evidences that Paul gives for Christ's resurrection.

Discuss: **When sharing the gospel with an unbeliever, what evidence can we give of Jesus' resurrection?**

OPTION ONE: (FOR A 90-MINUTE SESSION)

The Lord's Supper (15 Minutes)

Celebrate the Lord's Supper together using the words of institution found in 1 Corinthians 11:23-26. Then have volunteers read the following accounts of the Last Supper: Matthew 26:26-29; Mark 14:22-25; Luke 22:17-20. Discuss:

How are these accounts similar?

What is unique to each account?

What is most meaningful to you about celebrating the Lord's Supper?

What would make a person unworthy of participating in communion?

How should we examine ourselves before partaking (see 1 Corinthians 11:27-34)?

SECTION TWO: GOD'S PERSON (15 MINUTES)

BEING THE TEMPLE OF GOD'S SPIRIT

Objective: To discover how we are to be the temple of the Holy Spirit.

Read 1 Corinthians 3:9-17. Say: **Each Christian is to be filled with the Holy Spirit. With what does the Holy Spirit fill you?**

Have the group brainstorm about all the qualities and attributes of the Holy Spirit that indwell believers. Put their list on the board, flip chart or overhead. Now list all the fleshly qualities with which we fill ourselves. Discuss:

What wood, hay and stubble will the fire of God's Spirit burn away?

What work will last?

Form a circle. Have each person say to the one on his or her right and left, "I am the Church, you are the Church, we are the Church together." Then sing the hymn "The Church's One Foundation."

OPTION TWO: (FOR A 90-MINUTE SESSION)

Gifts in Christ's Church (15 Minutes)

Divide the group into three groups and assign the following passages:

Group One: 1 Corinthians 12:1-11
Group Two: 1 Corinthians 12:27-31
Group Three: 1 Corinthians 14:1-17,26-28

Ask each group to do the following (write the instructions on the board, flip chart or overhead):

List the gifts of the Holy Spirit mentioned in your assigned passage.

Describe briefly how those gifts are to be used in ministry to the Body of Christ.

After about five minutes, invite each group to share what they have discovered,

then with the whole group discuss:

What gifts operate in our local church body?

What makes for orderly and decent worship?

Why are the gifts important to the Church?

SECTION THREE: GOD'S SON (15 MINUTES)

JESUS CHRIST REVEALED AS OUR LORD

Objective: To see how Jesus is revealed as Our Lord in this book and to know Him as Lord over our daily lives.

In the Greek culture, wisdom—*sophia*—was worshiped as a god. The Cross was regarded as scandalous and foolish. Paul's preaching seemed simple and unintellectual to the Greeks. But Paul proclaimed Christ as the wisdom of God and the cross as evidence of God's power.

Divide the group into pairs. Have the pairs read 1 Corinthians 1:18—2:5. Ask them to complete the sentences on their handouts under the section entitled "Wisdom vs. Foolishness" and then share their responses with one another.

After they have shared about wisdom, say: **Paul wrote that Christ is both our Wisdom and our Lord, *kurios*. To be Lord is to be Master, Sovereign Ruler, over our lives. At times we try to control various areas of our lives. On your handouts, mark to what degree Jesus really is Lord over each area of your life. Pray for one another in your weakest areas.**

PURSUING GOD (5 MINUTES)

NEXT STEPS I NEED TO TAKE

Objective: To take a realistic assessment of one's relationship with Jesus and how that relationship might grow closer in the coming week.

Use 1 Corinthians 13 as a personal evaluation of members' relationships with the following groups of people (write the list on the board, flip chart or overhead):

The Lord

Their family

Other Christians

Unbelievers

In the same pairs, ask group members to share which characteristic of *agape* love found in 1 Corinthians 13 they need to exhibit most to the person(s) in each listed group. Have them identify the next step they will take in expressing that characteristic of love.

PRAYER (5 MINUTES)

Objective: To pray through the hymn of love in 1 Corinthians 13.

To close the session: while still in pairs, have them pray 1 Corinthians 13:4-8 for their partners. Give the following example for the pairs to get started:

Lord Jesus, empower _____ (name) _____ to love with patience, and with kindness, without envy, etc.

Close the prayer time by reading 1 Corinthians 15:54-57 as a benediction.

Session 9 Bible *Tuck-In*™

UNDERSTANDING 1 CORINTHIANS

The purpose of this session is:

- To provide an overview of Paul's first Epistle to the Corinthians;
- To discover how Jesus Christ is revealed in 1 Corinthians as our Lord.

KEY VERSES

"For the message of the cross is foolishness to those who are perishing, but to us who are being saved it is the power of God." 1 Corinthians 1:18

"Don't you know that you yourselves are God's temple and that God's Spirit lives in you?" 1 Corinthians 3:16

"The Lord Jesus, on the night he was betrayed, took bread, and when he had given thanks, he broke it and said, 'This is my body, which is for you; do this in remembrance of me.' In the same way, after supper he took the cup, saying, 'This cup is the new covenant in my blood; do this, whenever you drink it, in remembrance of me.'" 1 Corinthians 11:23-25

"There are different kinds of gifts, but the same Spirit. There

---

What makes for orderly and decent worship?
Why are the gifts important to the Church?

SECTION THREE: GOD'S SON (15 MINUTES)

JESUS CHRIST REVEALED AS OUR LORD

- Divide the group into pairs. Have the pairs read 1 Corinthians 1:18—2:5. Ask them to complete the handout section entitled "Wisdom vs. Foolishness" and then share their responses with one another.

- Have everyone complete "Jesus Is Lord over Every Area of Life" and then pray for their partner's weakest area.

PURSUING GOD (5 MINUTES)

NEXT STEPS I NEED TO TAKE

- Use 1 Corinthians 13 as a personal evaluation of members' relationships with the following groups of people: the Lord; their family; other Christians; unbelievers.

- In the same pairs, ask group members to share which characteristic of *agape* love found in 1 Corinthians 13 they need to exhibit most to the person(s) in each listed group. Have them identify the next step they will take in expressing that characteristic of love.

PRAYER (5 MINUTES)

- While still in pairs, have them pray 1 Corinthians 13:4-8 for their partners. Give the following example for the pairs to get started:
  Lord Jesus, empower _____ (name) _____ to love with patience, and with kindness, without envy, etc.

- Close the prayer time by reading 1 Corinthians 15:54-57 as a benediction.

are different kinds of service, but the same Lord. There are different kinds of working, but the same God works all of them in all men." 1 Corinthians 12:4-6

"If I speak in the tongues of men and of angels, but have not love, I am only a resounding gong or a clanging cymbal." 1 Corinthians 13:1

"And if Christ has not been raised, our preaching is useless and so is your faith." 1 Corinthians 15:14

SECTION ONE: GOD'S STORY (20 MINUTES)

GOD'S STORY IN 1 CORINTHIANS

- Greet everyone as they arrive. Tell the story, doing the suggested activities as you come to them. Distribute the handout "God's Story in 1 Corinthians" to group members.

OPTION ONE: (FOR A 90-MINUTE SESSION)

The Lord's Supper (15 Minutes)

- Celebrate the Lord's Supper together using 1 Corinthians 11:23-26. Then have volunteers read the following accounts of the Last Supper: Matthew 26:26-29; Mark 14:22-25; Luke 22:17-20. Discuss:

    How are these accounts similar? What is unique to each account?

    What is most meaningful to you about celebrating the Lord's Supper?

    What would make a person unworthy of participating in communion?

    How should we examine ourselves before partaking (see 1 Corinthians 11:27-34)?

SECTION TWO: GOD'S PERSON (15 MINUTES)

BEING THE TEMPLE OF GOD'S SPIRIT

- Read 1 Corinthians 3:9-17. Say: **Each Christian is to be filled with the Holy Spirit. With what does the Holy Spirit fill you?** Have the group brainstorm about all the qualities and attributes of the Holy Spirit that indwell believers. Put their list on the board, flip chart or overhead. Now list all the fleshly qualities with which we fill ourselves. Discuss: **What wood, hay and stubble will the fire of God's Spirit burn away? What work will last?**

- Form a circle. Have each person say to the one on his or her right and left, "I am the Church, you are the Church, we are the Church together." Then sing the hymn "The Church's One Foundation."

OPTION TWO: (FOR A 90-MINUTE SESSION)

Gifts in Christ's Church (15 Minutes)

- Divide the group into three groups and assign the following passages: Group One: 1 Corinthians 12:27-31; Group Two: 1 Corinthians 12:1-11; Group Three: 1 Corinthians 14:1-17,26-28. Ask each group to do the following (write the instructions on the board):

    List the gifts of the Holy Spirit mentioned in their passage.

    Describe briefly how those gifts are to be used in ministry to the Body of Christ.

- After about five minutes, invite each group to share what they have discovered, then with the whole group discuss: **What gifts operate in our local church body?**

GOD'S STORY IN 1 CORINTHIANS

1. The City of Corinth (1 Corinthians 1:2)

    Notes:

2. Corrections in Christian Conduct (1 Corinthians 1—11)

    Notes·

3. Instructions for Christian Conduct (1 Corinthians 12—16)

    Notes:

4. The Pillars of the Gospel (1 Corinthians 15)
    a. _____
    b. _____
    c. _____
    d. _____
    e. _____
    f. _____

WISDOM VS. FOOLISHNESS

Wisdom according to the world is…

CONTINUED

God's wisdom is...

To me, the cross of Christ means...

JESUS IS LORD OVER EVERY AREA OF LIFE

Shade in each area of your life to the degree that Jesus is really Lord over that area:

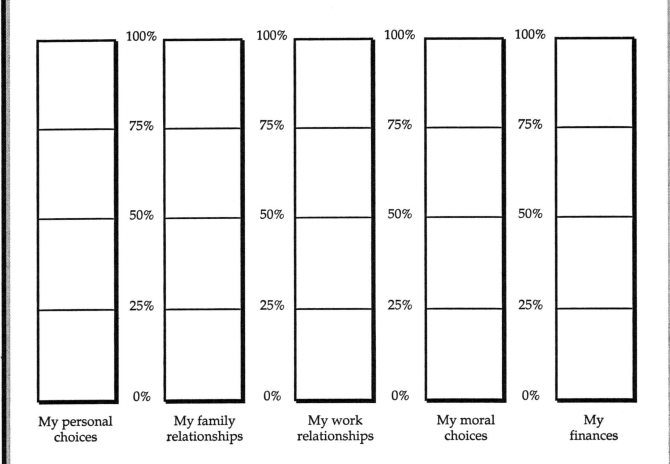

My personal choices   My family relationships   My work relationships   My moral choices   My finances

CONTINUED

Before the next session, read:

Sunday: Christ our Comfort (2 Corinthians 1:1—2:17)

Monday: Living Epistles (2 Corinthians 3:1—4:18)

Tuesday: Ambassadors for Christ (2 Corinthians 5:1—6:18)

Wednesday: The Heart of Paul (2 Corinthians 7:1—8:15)

Thursday: Christian Giving (2 Corinthians 8:16—9:15)

Friday: Paul's Apostleship (2 Corinthians 10:1—11:33)

Saturday: God's Strength (2 Corinthians 12:1—13:14)

Understanding 2 Corinthians

The purpose of this session is:
*   To provide an overview of Paul's second Epistle to the Corinthians;
*   To discover how Jesus Christ is revealed in 2 Corinthians as our Sufficiency.
In this session, group members will learn:
*   Key truths about God's story in 2 Corinthians;
*   How Jesus is revealed as our Sufficiency;
*   The basic principle that Christ provides all the tools and strength we need to fight the spiritual and physical battles we encounter;
*   How to apply the truths revealed in 2 Corinthians to their lives.

KEY VERSES

"Praise be to the God and Father of our Lord Jesus Christ, the Father of compassion and the God of all comfort, who comforts us in all our troubles, so that we can comfort those in any trouble with the comfort we ourselves have received from God." 2 Corinthians 1:3,4

"And we, who with unveiled faces all reflect the Lord's glory, are being transformed into his likeness with ever-increasing glory, which comes from the Lord, who is the Spirit." 2 Corinthians 3:18

"For you know the grace of our Lord Jesus Christ, that though he was rich, yet for your sakes he became poor, so that you through his poverty might become rich." 2 Corinthians 8:9

"For though we live in the world, we do not wage war as the world does. The weapons we fight with are not the weapons of the world. On the contrary, they have divine power to demolish strongholds. We demolish arguments and every pretension that sets itself up against the knowledge of God, and we take captive every thought to make it obedient to Christ." 2 Corinthians 10:3-5

"But [Jesus] said to me, 'My grace is sufficient for you, for my power is made perfect in weakness." 2 Corinthians 12:9

BEFORE THE SESSION

- Pray for group members by name, asking the Holy Spirit to reveal to them the spiritual truths in 2 Corinthians.
- Read chapter 35 of *What the Bible Is All About*.
- Prepare copies of Session 10 Handout, "God's Story in 2 Corinthians," for group members.
- Check off these supplies once you have secured them:
    - ____ A chalkboard and chalk or flip chart or overhead projector with markers.
    - ____ Extra Bibles, pencils and paper for group members.
    - ____ Three large sheets of poster board, several felt-tip pens and masking tape.
- If you are having a 90-minute session, carefully read the two option sections right now and pull together any supplies you need for them.
- Read the entire session and look up every passage. Have your Bible *Tuck-In*™ page ready.
- Arrive early and be ready to warmly greet each group member as he or she arrives.
- Memorize the key verses. Share them periodically and ask the group to repeat them as you teach the session.

SECTION ONE: GOD'S STORY (20 MINUTES)

GOD'S STORY IN 2 CORINTHIANS
Objective: To tell God's story so that Christians will apply the truths in 2 Corinthians to their own lives.

Greet everyone as they arrive. Tell the following story, doing the suggested activities as you come to them. Distribute the handout "God's Story in 2 Corinthians" to group members.

Introduction
Concerned about how the Corinthians received his first letter, Paul sent Timothy and perhaps Titus to the church in Corinth.

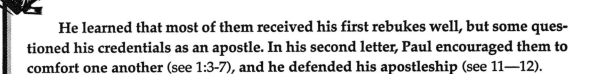

He learned that most of them received his first rebukes well, but some questioned his credentials as an apostle. In his second letter, Paul encouraged them to comfort one another (see 1:3-7), and he defended his apostleship (see 11—12).

Paul's Ministry (2 Corinthians 1—7)

The description that Paul gave of his ministry has provided a model for authentic ministry for the Church through the ages. Paul described those who ministered as being living letters for Christ and reflecting Jesus' image (see 3:1-6,18). He also stated that the gospel is a treasure in fragile "jars of clay"—our mortal bodies—to be shared with others no matter what the obstacles (see 4:1-12).

Divide the whole group into seven groups. Assign one of the first seven chapters to each group and have them survey their chapter to discover (write the following questions on the board, flip chart or overhead):

What is authentic ministry?

What obstacles will those in ministry face?

What comfort and joy does God give those in ministry?

Have the small groups share what they have discovered.

Giving Cheerfully (2 Corinthians 8—9)

Paul commended the Corinthian church for their generosity toward the churches experiencing famine in Palestine and encouraged them to give out of their poverty since Christ, though rich, became poor for their sakes (see 8:8; 9:6-11).

Have everyone complete the evaluation under point three of their handouts "Do I Have a Hang-Up with Giving?" After everyone has completed the survey, discuss:

What should be your motivation to give to the Lord?

What causes bad attitudes about giving?

What do you expect from God when you give?

What should you expect from Him?

Paul's Defense of His Ministry (2 Corinthians 10—13)

In the midst of defending himself as an apostle, Paul shares valuable insights about how Christ gives us spiritual weapons with which to fight (see 10:3-6); how Satan attacks and we should respond (see 11:14,15); and how Christ works in our lives in spite of our weaknesses (see 12:7-10).

Read 2 Corinthians 10:3-6 and 11:14,15 to the group, then discuss the following:

How do you take your thoughts captive when they begin to run wild with rebellion and sin?

How can you recognize when Satan is disguised as an angel of light?

What spiritual weapons can we use as Christians to defeat Satan's attacks and to strengthen one another?

OPTION ONE: (FOR A 90-MINUTE SESSION)

SELF-TESTING (15 MINUTES)

Read 2 Corinthians 13:5. Explain: **Paul urged the Corinthians to examine themselves spiritually. He told them they should not rely on past experiences or what they had done to validate their faith in Jesus. Rather, living in Christ is a daily walk with Him.**

Put the self-test questions on the board, flip chart or overhead. Have the group form pairs and then honestly answer the following questions with one another.

Do I love to think of Christ?
Do I love to pray?
Do I love to study God's Word?
Do I love Christian friends?
Do I love the Church?
Do I love to serve Christ?
Do I love my unsaved neighbors?

When they finish sharing, have them pray for one another to grow closer to Christ while being truthful about their spiritual walks with themselves and others.

SECTION TWO: GOD'S PERSON (15 MINUTES)

AN APOSTLE OF JESUS CHRIST

Objective: To discover what it means to be an apostle of Jesus Christ.

As an apostle and a missionary taking the gospel of Jesus Christ to the world, Paul encountered physical hardships and attacks both in the natural and spiritual realms. We can learn much about ourselves and God's ways by exploring Paul's apostleship.

Divide the group into three small groups and give each group a sheet of poster board and a few felt-tip pens. From their assigned passages, have each group draw a poster picturing the hardships that Paul faced. Assign the following passages to each group:

Group One: 2 Corinthians 4:7-18

Group Two: 2 Corinthians 6:3-10

Group Three: 2 Corinthians 11:16-33

After the groups finish, have each group share their posters with the whole group. Then discuss:

What hardships do Christians face when sharing the gospel in today's culture?

What are the most important lessons we can learn from Paul?

OPTION TWO: (FOR A 90-MINUTE SESSION)

His Grace Is Sufficient (15 Minutes)

Have the group read 2 Corinthians 12:9 in unison. Then ask each person to quietly meditate on this verse for five minutes following these instructions: **Get comfortable and put every other distracting thought out of your mind. Think only on the phrase "My grace is sufficient for you." Hear Jesus say that to you. As you say this verse over and over in your mind, emphasize a different word each time and think about what insights the Spirit gives you from that emphasis.**

Have everyone close their eyes and meditate on this verse for five minutes. After five minutes, discuss:

What did you hear the Lord saying to you as you meditated?

What is He saying to the Church?

Read 2 Corinthians 1:3-7. **How would He have us comfort one another in our times of weakness?**

How does Jesus use us to minister to one another with His strength and comfort?

SECTION THREE: GOD'S SON (15 MINUTES)

JESUS CHRIST REVEALED AS OUR SUFFICIENCY

Objective: To discover how Jesus is revealed in 2 Corinthians as our Sufficiency, and to understand how He meets our every need.

Read 2 Corinthians 12:1-10 to the group. Write the following topics on the board, flip chart or overhead and have the group suggest how Christ meets our needs when we are:

Poor	Sick	Hurting
Hungry	Lost	Lonely

Then discuss:

Why does Christ choose to work through our weakness?

How does our pride get in the way of Him working in us?

PURSUING GOD (5 MINUTES)

NEXT STEPS I NEED TO TAKE

Objective: To take a realistic assessment of one's relationship with Jesus and how that relationship might grow closer in the coming week.

Ask everyone to find a partner and sit down with him or her face-to-face. Have each person read 2 Corinthians 3:1-6 to the partner. Invite each person to write a letter to someone explaining what Jesus means to him or her. Then instruct the partners to read their letters to one another.

PRAYER (5 MINUTES)

Objective: To pray for one another to become the living letters Paul writes about us becoming in 2 Corinthians 3.

With the same pairs, have the partners pray for one another to become more like Christ in the way that they wrote in their letters.

Have the group form a circle. Read 2 Corinthians 12:9 to the group. Have each group member express his or her thanks to Christ by praying, **"When I am weak, Jesus ..."**

Session 10 Bible *Tuck-In*™

UNDERSTANDING 2 CORINTHIANS

The purpose of this session is:

- To provide an overview of Paul's second Epistle to the Corinthians;
- To discover how Jesus Christ is revealed in 2 Corinthians as our Sufficiency.

KEY VERSES

"Praise be to the God and Father of our Lord Jesus Christ, the Father of compassion and the God of all comfort, who comforts us in all our troubles, so that we can comfort those in any trouble with the comfort we ourselves have received from God." 2 Corinthians 1:3,4

"And we, who with unveiled faces all reflect the Lord's glory, are being transformed into his likeness with ever-increasing glory, which comes from the Lord, who is the Spirit." 2 Corinthians 3:18

"For you know the grace of our Lord Jesus Christ, that though he was rich, yet for your sakes he became poor, so that you through his poverty might become rich." 2 Corinthians 8:9

"For though we live in the world, we do not wage war as

How does Jesus use us to minister His strength and comfort to one another as members of His Body?

SECTION THREE: GOD'S SON (15 MINUTES)

JESUS CHRIST REVEALED AS OUR SUFFICIENCY

- Read 2 Corinthians 12:1-10 to the group. Write the following topics on the board, flip chart or overhead and have the group suggest how Christ meets our needs when we are:

  Poor   Sick   Hurting
  Hungry   Lost   Lonely

- Then discuss:

  Why does Christ choose to work in our weakness?
  How does our pride get in the way of His working in us?

PURSUING GOD (5 MINUTES)

NEXT STEPS I NEED TO TAKE

- Ask everyone to find a partner and sit down face-to-face. Have each person read 2 Corinthians 3:1-6 to the partner. Give everyone a piece of paper, a pen or pencil and invite them to write a letter to someone explaining what Jesus means to him or her. Then instruct the partners to read their letters to one another.

PRAYER (5 MINUTES)

- With the same pairs, have the partners pray for one another to become more like Christ in the way that they wrote in their letters.

- Have the group form a circle. Read 2 Corinthians 12:9 to the group. Have each group member express his or her thanks to Christ by praying "When I am weak, Jesus …"

the world does. The weapons we fight with are not the weapons of the world. On the contrary, they have divine power to demolish strongholds. We demolish arguments and every pretension that sets itself up against the knowledge of God, and we take captive every thought to make it obedient to Christ." 2 Corinthians 10:3-5

"But [Jesus] said to me, 'My grace is sufficient for you, for my power is made perfect in weakness.'" 2 Corinthians 12:9

SECTION ONE: GOD'S STORY (20 MINUTES)

GOD'S STORY IN 2 CORINTHIANS

• Greet everyone as they arrive. Tell the story, doing the suggested activities as you come to them. Distribute the handout "God's Story in 2 Corinthians" to group members.

OPTION ONE: (FOR A 90-MINUTE SESSION)

Self-Testing (15 Minutes)

• Read 2 Corinthians 13:5 to the group.
• Write the self-test questions on the board, flip chart or overhead. Have pairs honestly answer the questions with their partners. Then have them pray for one another to grow closer to Christ while being truthful about their spiritual walks with themselves and others.

Do I love to think of Christ?

Do I love to study God's Word?

Do I love the Church?

Do I love my unsaved neighbors?

Do I love to pray?

Do I love Christian friends?

Do I love Christ?

Do I love to serve Christ?

SECTION TWO: GOD'S PERSON (15 MINUTES)

AN APOSTLE OF JESUS CHRIST

• Explain what an apostle is. Divide the group into three small groups and give each group a sheet of poster board and a few felt-tip pens. From their assigned passages, have each group draw a poster picturing the hardships that Paul faced. Assign the following passages to each group: Group One: 2 Corinthians 4:7-18; Group Two: 2 Corinthians 6:3-10; Group Three: 2 Corinthians 11:16-33.

• After the groups finish, have each group share their posters with the whole group. Then discuss:

What hardships do Christians face when sharing the gospel in today's culture?
What are the most important lessons we can learn from Paul?

OPTION TWO: (FOR A 90-MINUTE SESSION)

His Grace Is Sufficient (15 Minutes)

• Read 2 Corinthians 12:9 in unison. Then ask each person to quietly meditate on this verse for five minutes following these instructions: Get comfortable and put every other distracting thought out of your mind. Think only on the phrase "My grace is sufficient for you." Hear Jesus say that to you. As you say this verse over and over in your mind, emphasize a different word each time and think about what insights the Spirit gives you from that emphasis.

• After five minutes, discuss:
What did you hear the Lord saying to you as you meditated?
What is He saying to the Church?
Read 2 Corinthians 1:3-7. How would He have us comfort one another in our times of weakness?

Fold

GOD'S STORY IN 2 CORINTHIANS

1. Introduction

   Notes:

2. Paul's Ministry (2 Corinthians 1—7)

   Notes:

3. Giving Cheerfully (2 Corinthians 8—9)

   Notes:

DO I HAVE A HANG-UP WITH GIVING?

Circle the attitudes you usually have when you give to the Lord:

Joyful	Dutiful	Excited about the coming harvest
Expectant	Grateful to God	Begrudging Reluctant
Cheerful	Compassionate	Loving

CONTINUED

4. Paul's Defense of His Ministry (2 Corinthians 10—13)

Notes:

Before the next session, read:
Sunday: Only One Gospel (Galatians 1:1-24)
Monday: Justified by Faith (Galatians 2:1-21)
Tuesday: The Law Points to Christ (Galatians 3:1-29)
Wednesday: Law and Grace (Galatians 4:1-31)
Thursday: Stand Fast in Christian Liberty (Galatians 5:1-16)
Friday: Flesh versus Spirit (Galatians 5:17-26)
Saturday: Sowing and Reaping (Galatians 6:1-18)

Understanding Galatians

The purpose of this session is:
- To provide an overview of Paul's epistle to the Galatians;
- To discover how Jesus Christ is revealed in Galatians as our Liberty.

In this session, group members will learn:
- Key truths about God's story in Galatians;
- That Jesus is revealed as our Liberty;
- The basic principles that the power of Jesus' death on the cross frees us from the curse of the law and that grace is the undeserved and unearned gift of salvation from God;
- How to apply the truths revealed in Galatians to their daily lives.

KEY VERSES

"For through the law I died to the law so that I might live for God. I have been crucified with Christ and I no longer live, but Christ lives in me. The life I live in the body, I live by faith in the Son of God, who loved me and gave himself for me." Galatians 2:19,20

"You are all sons of God through faith in Christ Jesus, for all of you who were baptized into Christ have clothed yourselves with Christ. There is neither Jew nor Greek, slave nor free, male nor female, for you are all one in Christ Jesus." Galatians 3:26-28

"It is for freedom that Christ has set us free. Stand firm, then, and do not let yourselves be burdened again by a yoke of slavery." Galatians 5:1

"Do not be deceived: God cannot be mocked. A man reaps what he sows. The one who sows to please his sinful nature, from that nature will reap destruction; the one who sows to please the Spirit, from the Spirit will reap eternal life." Galatians 6:7,8

BEFORE THE SESSION

- Pray for group members by name, asking the Holy Spirit to reveal to them the spiritual truths in Galatians.
- Read chapter 36 of *What the Bible Is All About*.
- Prepare copies of Session 11 handout "God's Story in Galatians" for group members.

- Check off these supplies once you have secured them:
  - ____ A chalkboard and chalk or flip chart or overhead projector with markers.
  - ____ Extra Bibles, pencils and paper for group members.
  - ____ Long, sharp nails for everyone in the group, and a wastepaper basket.
  - ____ A package of sunflower or pumpkin seeds with enough seeds for everyone in the group to have at least one.
  - ____ Purple construction paper, black felt-tip pens and pencils.
- If you are having a 90-minute session, carefully read the two option sections right now and pull together any supplies you need for them.
- Read the entire session and look up every passage. Have your Bible *Tuck-In*™ page ready.
- Arrive early and be ready to warmly greet each group member as he or she arrives.
- Memorize the key verses. Share them periodically and ask the group to repeat them as you teach the session.

SECTION ONE: GOD'S STORY (20 MINUTES)

GOD'S STORY IN GALATIANS

Objective: To tell God's story so that Christians will apply the truths in Galatians to their own lives.

Greet everyone as they arrive. Tell the following story, doing the suggested activities as you come to them. Distribute the handout "God's Story in Galatians" to group members.

Introduction (Galatians 1:1-11)

During Paul's second missionary journey (see Acts 16:6), he was delayed in Galatia by illness and while there he established a church. This rural area was filled with itinerant preachers and teachers who didn't follow Paul's teaching. They taught that new Christians needed to be circumcised and that they must follow Jewish Law. They discredited Paul, saying he wasn't one of the original disciples and had no authority as an apostle. So Paul wrote to the Galatians that they should lift up Christ's crucifixion as the event that set them free from the curse of sin and the law (see Galatians 3:10-14).

Read Galatians 1:1-11 to the group and then discuss:

What can we learn about Paul personally from this text?

What is Paul's central concern in the introduction of this letter?

Christ, Our Deliverer and Savior

The theme of Paul's letter is "Christ crucified" or "the power of the cross." Jesus died on the cross as the Savior of the world to free us from sin and the curse of the Law. Paul contrasted law and grace (see Galatians 5). Grace, *charis*, is the undeserved and unearned gift of salvation from God. Beginning with Galatians 1:4, Paul declared what Christ the Savior had done through the power of the cross (see 1:3,4; 2:20,21; 3:13,21,22).

Assign the following passages to various group members. After each passage is read aloud to the group, have a volunteer summarize with a word or phrase how that passage describes the way in which Jesus delivers us through the power of His death on the cross. Write a summary phrase on the board, flip chart or overhead next to the corresponding verse.

> **Galatians 1:3,4** (To deliver us from sin)
> **Galatians 3:13** (To deliver us from the curse of the law)
> **Galatians 2:20** (To deliver us from self-centeredness)
> **Galatians 6:14** (To deliver us from the world)
> **Galatians 3:14** (To give us the Holy Spirit)
> **Galatians 5:22-25** (To give us the fruit of the Holy Spirit)

Paul Defended His Apostleship (Galatians 1:12—2:21)

Paul shared his experience of being called by Christ and described his confrontation with Peter. He had personally experienced justification by faith through God's grace and had been called by God to declare that message to others, being accepted and sent out by the disciples themselves (see Galatians 2:1-10).

Divide the whole group into four groups and assign each group one of the following passages:

> Group One—Paul's Calling (Galatians 1:11-24)
> Group Two—Paul's Commissioning (Galatians 2:1-10)
> Group Three—Paul's Confrontation with Peter (Galatians 2:11-16)
> Group Four—Paul's Crucifixion with Christ (Galatians 2:17-21)

Instruct each group to write a short summary of Paul's experience from their assigned passage. They may present it to the group in a brief drama or a reader's theater where actors silently act while a narrator reads the story.

Paul Defended the Gospel (Galatians 3:1—4:31)

Legalists try to make good news into bad news. The good news is that God has set us free from sin, from the curse of the law and from death through our

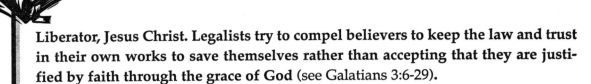

Liberator, Jesus Christ. Legalists try to compel believers to keep the law and trust in their own works to save themselves rather than accepting that they are justified by faith through the grace of God (see Galatians 3:6-29).

Read Galatians 3:10-29 to the group. Give everyone a nail, a pen or pencil and a piece of paper. Ask each person to write on that paper their sins that Jesus died for. After a few minutes, instruct the group members to fold their paper several times and then push the nail through it, symbolizing that Jesus broke the curse of sin through the cross. Have them throw away the nail and paper to symbolize that past sin has now been released and discarded from their lives.

Paul Desired that the Gospel Be Applied (Galatians 5—6)

The Cross has liberated us from the control of sin (see 5:1). We are to stand firm in our liberty and not abuse our freedom by a lack of love (see 5:13-15) or by unclean living (see 5:16-26). Rather we are to exhibit the fruit of the Spirit (see 5:22-26) and to sow to the Spirit in our lives (see 6:7-10).

Ask everyone to write Galatians 5:1 and 5:6 on their handouts under point five as you write those texts on the board, flip chart or overhead. As a group, discuss:
How do Christians today burden themselves with legalism?
What are some unwritten laws in our church from which we need to be liberated because they are simply the traditions of men?
How can we express faith through love to one another in practical ways?

OPTION ONE: (FOR A 90-MINUTE SESSION)

The Fruit of the Spirit (15 Minutes)

Read Galatians 5:22,23. Discuss what each fruit means.

Give everyone purple construction paper, a pen or pencil, and black felt-tip pens. Ask everyone to draw a cluster of nine grapes on their papers. They can use quarters to draw the circles for the nine grapes. Have them write the name of a different fruit of the spirit from Galatians 5:22,23 next to each grape.

Have everyone find a partner, then give the following instructions: **Shade the inside of each grape to the point that that particular fruit is being produced in your life. For example, if that fruit is only expressed about half the time in your life, then shade it in halfway. After each of you have shaded your grapes, share with one another how you have responded and where you need to allow the Holy Spirit to work more deeply in your life. Then pray for one another.**

SECTION TWO: GOD'S PERSON (15 MINUTES)

THE CHRISTIAN: FREE IN CHRIST!

Objective: To discover our freedom and identity as one in Christ.

Ask everyone to read Galatians 5:1-15. Have the group brainstorm all of the things that keep us from being free in Christ. List those things on the board, flip chart or overhead.

Ask the group members to fill out the checklist on their handouts entitled "Free In Christ!"

OPTION TWO: (FOR A 90-MINUTE SESSION)

Sowing and Reaping (15 Minutes)

Bring a bag of small candy bars. Ask for one volunteer who will eat just one piece of candy. After the person eats one of the small candy bars, ask him or her how many of these he or she could eat each day over the next week before gaining one pound. Say: **We could eat just one of these today and probably get away with it. But one each day for the next week or month will begin to bring a harvest of additional pounds on our bodies. What is the lie we could tell ourselves if we wanted to eat these?**

Read Galatians 6:7-10 to the group. As a group, list all the good seeds that Christians can sow and the harvest we can expect. Also, list the bad seeds we might be tempted to sow and the harvest we can expect from that.

SECTION THREE: GOD'S SON (15 MINUTES)

JESUS CHRIST REVEALED AS OUR LIBERTY

Objective: To see how Jesus is revealed in Galatians as the One who sets us free.

Jesus has set us free from the law and the curse of sin and death to live according to the Spirit of God. We have been set free by His grace from the acts of the sinful nature.

Read Galatians 5:16-21 slowly to the group and ask each person to list on the back of their handouts each act of sin that Paul mentions. Discuss the meaning of each sinful act, making certain that each person knows what each sin really is. The following is a list of the words with definitions or synonyms to help understand the acts of the sinful nature:

1. Adultery: having sexual intercourse with a person other than one's spouse.
2. Fornication: having sexual intercourse outside of marriage.
3. Uncleanness: impurity, immorality.
4   Licentiousness: wantonness, lewdness, sensuality and runaway passion for pleasure and violence.
5. Idolatry: worshiping anything as a god.
6. Sorcery: witchcraft, involvement with magic, new age or cultic practices, horoscopes, psychics, etc.
7. Murders, hatred, fits of rage, selfish ambition, dissentions, factions and envy: acts of selfishness and violence against others.
8. Drunkenness, orgies and the like: addiction, sexual pleasures, pornography and materialism.

Ask each person to cross out those acts of sin that the Spirit has completely eradicated from their lives. Underline those sinful acts that the Holy Spirit is dealing with right now in their lives. Then have them write a prayer asking the Holy Spirit to cleanse and liberate them from that sin through Jesus' shed blood.

Pursuing God (5 Minutes)

Next Steps I Need to Take

Objective: To take a realistic assessment of one's relationship with Jesus and how that relationship might grow closer in the coming week.

Have everyone read Galatians 6:7-10. Give everyone a seed. Allow each person time to think about the kind of seed they want to sow in the Spirit. Let each person share the kind of seed they desire to sow in God's kingdom.

Prayer (5 Minutes)

Objective: To pray for liberty in Christ for one another.

Read Galatians 5:1 and John 8:32. Say: **In Galatians, we learned that the law reveals sin but does not remove it. The law puts us into bondage, but Christ has set us free from the curse of the law. Let's pray for true liberty in God's Spirit through the blood of Jesus Christ.**

Invite group members to form a circle and pray as they are led, giving thanks for the liberty we have in Christ Jesus. Close with a prayer of thanksgiving for freedom in Christ, our Liberator.

Pursuing God (5 Minutes)

Next Steps I Need to Take

- Have everyone read Galatians 6:7-10. Give everyone a seed. Allow everyone time to think about the kind of seed they want to sow in the Spirit. Let each person share the kind of seed he or she desires to sow in God's kingdom.

Prayer (5 Minutes)

- Read Galatians 5:1 and John 8:32. Invite group members to form a circle and pray as they are led, giving thanks for the liberty we have in Christ Jesus. Close with a prayer of thanksgiving for freedom in Christ, our Liberator.

Session 11 Bible *Tuck-In*™

UNDERSTANDING GALATIANS

The purpose of this session is:

- To provide an overview of Paul's Epistle to the Galatians;
- To discover how Jesus Christ is revealed in Galatians as our Liberty.

Key Verses

"For through the law I died to the law so that I might live for God. I have been crucified with Christ and I no longer live, but Christ lives in me. The life I live in the body, I live by faith in the Son of God, who loved me and gave himself for me." Galatians 2:19,20

"You are all sons of God through faith in Christ Jesus, for all of you who were baptized into Christ have clothed yourselves with Christ. There is neither Jew nor Greek, slave nor free, male nor female, for you are all one in Christ Jesus." Galatians 3:26-28

"It is for freedom that Christ has set us free. Stand firm, then, and do not let yourselves be burdened again by a yoke of slavery." Galatians 5:1

"Do not be deceived: God cannot be mocked. A man reaps what he sows. The one who sows to please his sinful nature,

"from that nature will reap destruction; the one who sows to please the Spirit, from the Spirit will reap eternal life."
Galatians 6:7,8

SECTION ONE: GOD'S STORY (20 MINUTES)

GOD'S STORY IN GALATIANS

- Greet everyone as they arrive. Tell the story of Galatians, doing the suggested activities as you come to them. Distribute the handout "God's Story in Galatians" to group members.

OPTION ONE: (FOR A 90-MINUTE SESSION)

The Fruit of the Spirit (15 Minutes)

- Read Galatians 5:22,23. Discuss what each fruit means.
- Give everyone purple construction paper, a pen or pencil, and black felt-tip pens. Ask everyone to draw a cluster of nine grapes on their papers. They can use quarters to draw the circles for the nine grapes. Have them write the name of a different fruit of the spirit from Galatians 5:22,23 next to each grape. Have everyone find a partner and give the instructions.

SECTION TWO: GOD'S PERSON (15 MINUTES)

THE CHRISTIAN: FREE IN CHRIST!

- Ask everyone to read Galatians 5:1-15. Have the group brainstorm all the kinds of things that keep us from being free in Christ. List those things on the board, flip chart or overhead.
- Ask the group members to fill out the check list on their handouts entitled "Free In Christ!"

-- Fold --

OPTION TWO: (FOR A 90-MINUTE SESSION)

Sowing and Reaping (15 Minutes)

- Bring a bag of small candy bars. Ask for one volunteer who will eat just one piece of candy. After the person eats one of the small candy bars, ask him or her how many of these he or she could eat each day over the next week before gaining one pound.
- Read Galatians 6:7-10 to the group. As a group, list all the good seeds that Christians can sow and the harvest we can expect. Also, list the bad seeds we might be tempted to sow and the harvest we can expect from that.

SECTION THREE: GOD'S SON (15 MINUTES)

JESUS CHRIST REVEALED AS OUR LIBERTY

- Slowly read Galatians 5:16-21 to the group and ask each person to list on the back of their handouts each act of sin that Paul mentions. Discuss the meaning of each sinful act making certain that each person knows what each sin really is.
- Ask each person to cross out those acts of sin that the Spirit has completely eradicated from their lives. Underline those sinful acts that the Holy Spirit is dealing with right now in their lives. Then have them write a prayer asking the Holy Spirit to cleanse and liberate them from that sin through Jesus' shed blood.

GOD'S STORY IN GALATIANS

1. Introduction (Galatians 1:1-11)

   Notes:

2. Christ, Our Deliverer and Savior

   Notes:

3. Paul Defended His Apostleship (Galatians 1:12—2:21).

   Notes:

4. Paul Defended the Gospel (Galatians 3:1—4:31).

   Notes:

5. Paul Desired that the Gospel Be Applied (Galatians 5—6).

   Notes:

CONTINUED

Galatians 5:1—

Galatians 5:6—

FREE IN CHRIST!

Check all the things in your past from which Christ has set you free.

_____	Guilt	_____	Rejection
_____	Sin	_____	Fear
_____	Pain	_____	Depression
_____	Hurt	_____	Addiction
_____	Grief	_____	Unresolved anger

Before next session, read:
Sunday: The Believer's Position (Ephesians 1:1-23)
Monday: Saved by Grace (Ephesians 2:1-22)
Tuesday: A Mystery Revealed (Ephesians 3:1-21)
Wednesday: A Christian's Walk (Ephesians 4:1-32)
Thursday: Following Christ (Ephesians 5:1-20)
Friday: Living with Others (Ephesians 5:21—6:9)
Saturday: Christian Warfare (Ephesians 6:10-24)

Understanding Ephesians

The purpose of this session is:
- To provide an overview of Paul's Epistle to the Ephesians;
- To discover how Jesus Christ is revealed in Ephesians as our All-in-All.

In this session, group members will learn:
- Key truths about God's story in Ephesians;
- That Jesus is revealed as our All-in-All;
- The basic principle that Christ is the Head of the Church and that His Body is made up of the saints;
- How to apply the truths revealed in Ephesians to our daily lives.

KEY VERSES

"For it is by grace you have been saved, through faith—and this not from yourselves, it is the gift of God—not by works, so that no one can boast." Ephesians 2:8,9

"And in him you too are being built together to become a dwelling in which God lives by his Spirit." Ephesians 2:22

"And I pray that you, being rooted and established in love, may have power, together with all the saints, to grasp how wide and long and high and deep is the love of Christ, and to know this love that surpasses knowledge—that you may be filled to the measure of all the fullness of God." Ephesians 3:17-19

"Finally, be strong in the Lord and in his mighty power. Put on the full armor of God so that you can take your stand against the devil's schemes." Ephesians 6:10,11

BEFORE THE SESSION

- Pray for group members by name, asking the Holy Spirit to reveal to them the spiritual truths in Ephesians.
- Read chapter 37 in *What the Bible Is All About*.
- Prepare copies of Session 12 handouts "God's Story in Ephesians" and "The Full Armor of God" for all group members.
- Check off these supplies once you have secured them:

_____ A chalkboard and chalk or flip chart or overhead projector with markers.

_____ Extra Bibles, pencils and paper for group members.

_____ 3x5-inch index cards, one for each group member.

- If you are having a 90-minute session, carefully read the two option sections right now and pull together any supplies you need for them.

- Read the entire session and look up every passage. Have your Bible *Tuck-In™* page ready.

- Arrive early and be ready to warmly greet each group member as he or she arrives.

- Memorize the key verses. Share them periodically and ask the group to repeat them as you teach the session.

SECTION ONE: GOD'S STORY (20 MINUTES)

GOD'S STORY IN EPHESIANS

Objective: To tell God's story so that Christians will apply the truths in Ephesians to their own lives.

Greet everyone as they arrive. Tell the following story, doing the suggested activities as you come to them. Distribute the handout "God's Story in Ephesians" to all the group members.

Introduction (Ephesians 1:1-10)

In Ephesians, Paul wrote about the great mystery of the Church, the Body of Christ. God the Father not only prepared a physical body for Jesus Christ to suffer in, but He prepared a Body—the Church—in which He could be glorified. Church, *ecclesia*, means an "assembly of called-out ones." The Church is an organism, not an organization—its Body is made up of the saints and its Head is Christ (see Galatians 1:1-10).

Discuss: **How is the Church called to be different from the world?**

The Holy Temple of the Lord (Ephesians 2:21)

Ephesians is masterfully constructed to reveal Christ's Temple with six magnificent rooms which we will explore together. In Christ's Body—His Church—the believer comes to understand both his position and the condition of his walk in Christ (see Ephesians 1:15-23).

Have the group members think about your own church facility. List the different rooms in your church. Identify the kinds of ministry done in each room. Say: **Just as the various rooms of our church's physical facilities are built to provide for different kinds of ministry, so the spiritual Church has different "rooms" for ministry. Let's explore those rooms together through the book of Ephesians.**

The Anteroom (Ephesians 1)

As we enter Christ's Temple, we discover the bountiful blessings apportioned to us as believers and as saints (see Ephesians 1:1—2:13). We also uncover how God redeemed us—brought us over from sin to salvation—through Christ (see 1:4-14).

Invite any group members who wish to share how Christ has redeemed them and saved them. Keep the testimonies to just two or three brief sentences.

The Audience Chamber of the King (Ephesians 2)

We are sitting together with Christ in the heavenly places (see 2:1,6). In His presence, we are being changed and transformed as His workmanship (see 2:10). In Christ, we will receive the incomparable riches of His grace (see 2:7).

Give each person a 3x5-inch index card. Ask everyone to write a confession on their cards about one way that they often try to earn God's favor and salvation instead of simply accepting His grace. Read Ephesians 2:8,9 in unison. Then invite group members to tear up their cards as an active commitment to themselves to remove the "works" salvation mentality from their lives.

The Throne Room (Ephesians 3)

In Christ, we have the boldness to approach the throne of God with confidence through faith (see 3:12). Gentiles and Jews alike who trust in Christ can come before His throne as one people (see 2:11-22).

One way we boldly approach the throne of God is through prayer. With the whole group, spend about three minutes in prayer, thanking God for the privilege of being able to approach His throne boldly through the shed blood of Jesus.

The Jewel Room (Ephesians 4)

A gift of grace (see 4:7) is given to each believer that is to be used to God's glory for the equipping of the saints (see 4:12,13).
Ask each person to share his or her completion of the following statement:
One gift in the church for which I'm thankful is …

The Choir and Oratory Room (Ephesians 5)

The members of Christ's Body worship and praise Him as they are filled with the Spirit (see 5:18-20).

Have the group select a hymn or chorus that they all know. Sing it together in worship and praise of Christ.

The Armory (Ephesians 6)

His saints have the whole armor of God and prayer to withstand the enemy's attacks and to experience victory (see 6:10-20).

Have the group help you make an intercessory prayer list on the board and invite group members to make their own lists and pray for the requests during the week.

OPTION ONE: (FOR A 90-MINUTE SESSION)

Equipping the Saints (15 Minutes)

Divide the whole group into five small groups. Read Ephesians 4:11-16. Assign each group one of the following equipping gifts: apostles, prophets, evangelists, pastors or teachers. Have each small group spend five minutes brainstorming all the ways that particular gift equips the saints to minister the gospel.

Bring the whole group back together and share what each has discovered. After all groups have shared, discuss: **How can we be more effective in equipping the saints in our church?**

SECTION TWO: GOD'S PERSON (15 MINUTES)

THE SAINT: MIGHTY WARRIOR ARMED WITH GOD'S ARMOR

Objective: To discover how we as saints can be equipped with God's armor to withstand the enemy's attacks and pray victoriously.

Give each group member a copy of handout 2 "The Full Armor of God." Ask each person to read Ephesians 6:10-18 and to fill in the parts of the armor on the warrior. Divide into pairs and ask the partners to share which part of the armor is

strongest in their lives and which is weakest. Have the partners pray for one another: for each part of the armor to be strengthened through Christ.

OPTION TWO: (FOR A 90-MINUTE SESSION)

RECONCILED IN CHRIST (15 MINUTES)

Read Ephesians 2:11-22. Group members will explore ways that Christ reconciles persons who may be at enmity with one another. Carefully consider each form of enmity. List on the board, flip chart or overhead all of the ways that Christ would bring about reconciliation in that kind of relationship. Then pray as a group for each area needing reconciliation.

> **Different ethnic groups**
> **Estranged family members**
> **Hurt church members**
> **National enemies**
> **Political opponents**
> **Victims and abusers**

SECTION THREE: GOD'S SON (15 MINUTES)

JESUS CHRIST REVEALED AS OUR ALL-IN-ALL

Objective: To see how Jesus is revealed in Ephesians as Our All-in-All, meeting every need.

Paul used the analogy of marriage to describe the relationship of Christ and the church. Let's see how Christ meets our needs just as husbands and wives should meet one another's needs in marriage.

Divide the group into men and women. Have each group read Ephesians 5:22-33 and make two lists: one titled "His Needs" and one titled "Her Needs."

Encourage the groups to apply the verses to their own experiences and to be as practical as possible in their lists. After about seven minutes, bring the men and women back together. Have a representative from each group write their respective lists on the board, flip chart or overhead. Option: If your group consists of all women or all men, have the whole group work together on the two lists. Then discuss:

How does Jesus as the Bridegroom of the Church meet our every need in the church community?

What are some ways the Church might try to meet needs instead of letting Christ meet the needs?

PURSUING GOD (5 MINUTES)

NEXT STEPS I NEED TO TAKE

Objective: To take a realistic assessment of one's relationship with Jesus and how that relationship might grow closer in the coming week.

Have the group form pairs and read Ephesians 4:17-32. Ask each partner to identify one or two verses that convict him or her about the ways he or she needs to grow in his or her relationship with Christ. Have the partners share those verses with one another and what the Lord is saying to each one through those verses.

PRAYER (5 MINUTES)

Objective: To pray for the group members the way Paul prayed for the Ephesians in chapter three.

Have the group turn to Ephesians 3:16-21 and read this prayer in unison to close the session.

What are some ways the Church might try to meet needs instead of letting Christ meet the needs?

Pursuing God (5 Minutes)

Next Steps I Need to Take

- Have the group form pairs and read Ephesians 4:17-32. Ask each partner to identify one or two verses that convict him or her about the ways he or she needs to grow in his or her relationship with Christ. Have the partners share those verses with one another and what the Lord is saying to each one through those verses.

Prayer (5 Minutes)

- Have the group turn to Ephesians 3:16-21 and read this prayer in unison to close the session.

---Fold---

Session 12 Bible *Tuck-In™*

UNDERSTANDING EPHESIANS

The purpose of this session is:

- To provide an overview of Paul's Epistle to the Ephesians;
- To discover how Jesus Christ is revealed in Ephesians as our All-in-All.

Key Verses

"For it is by grace you have been saved, through faith—and this not from yourselves, it is the gift of God—not by works, so that no one can boast." Ephesians 2:8,9

"And in him you too are being built together to become a dwelling in which God lives by his Spirit." Ephesians 2:22

"And I pray that you, being rooted and established in love, may have power, together with all the saints, to grasp how wide and long and high and deep is the love of Christ, and to know this love that surpasses knowledge—that you may be filled to the measure of all the fullness of God." Ephesians 3:17-19

"Finally, be strong in the Lord and in his mighty power. Put on the full armor of God so that you can take your stand against the devil's schemes." Ephesians 6:10,11

SECTION ONE: GOD'S STORY (20 MINUTES)

GOD'S STORY IN EPHESIANS

• Greet everyone as they arrive. Tell the story of Ephesians, doing the suggested activities as you come to them. Distribute the handout "God's Story in Ephesians" to all group members.

OPTION ONE: (FOR A 90-MINUTE SESSION)

EQUIPPING THE SAINTS (15 MINUTES)

• Divide the whole group into five small groups. Read Ephesians 4:11-16. Assign each group one of the following equipping gifts: apostles, prophets, evangelists, pastors or teachers. Have each small group spend five minutes brainstorming all the ways that particular gift equips the saints to minister the gospel.

• Bring the whole group back together and share what each has discovered. After all groups have shared, discuss: **How can we be more effective in equipping the saints in our church?**

SECTION TWO: GOD'S PERSON (15 MINUTES)

THE SAINTS: MIGHTY WARRIORS ARMED WITH GOD'S ARMOR

• Give each group member a copy of handout 2 "The Full Armor of God." Ask each person to read Ephesians 6:10-18 and to fill in the parts of the armor on the warrior. Divide into pairs and ask the partners to share which part of the armor is strongest in their lives and which is weakest. Have the partners pray for one another: for each part of the armor to be strengthened through Christ.

OPTION TWO: (FOR A 90-MINUTE SESSION)

Reconciled in Christ (15 Minutes)

• Read Ephesians 2:11-22. Group members will explore ways that Christ reconciles persons who may be at enmity with one another. Carefully consider each form of enmity. List on the board, flip chart or overhead all of the ways that Christ would bring about reconciliation in that kind of relationship. Then pray as a group for each area needing reconciliation.

> Different ethnic groups
> Estranged family members
> Hurt church members
> National enemies
> Political opponents
> Victims and abusers

SECTION THREE: GOD'S SON (15 MINUTES)

JESUS CHRIST REVEALED AS OUR ALL-IN-ALL

• Divide the group into men and women. Have each group read Ephesians 5:22-33 and make two lists: one titled "His Needs" and one titled "Her Needs." Encourage the groups to apply the verses to their own experiences and to be as practical as possible in their lists. After about seven minutes, bring the men and women back together. Have a representative from each group write their respective lists on the board, flip chart or overhead. Option: If your group consists of all women or all men, have the whole group work together on the two lists. Then discuss: **How does Jesus as the Bridegroom of the Church meet our every need in the church community?**

GOD'S STORY IN EPHESIANS

1. Introduction (Ephesians 1:1-10)

   Notes:

2. The Holy Temple of the Lord (Ephesians 2:21)

   Notes:

3. The Anteroom (Ephesians 1)

   Notes:

4. The Audience Chamber of the King (Ephesians 2)

   Notes:

5. The Throne Room (Ephesians 3)

   Notes:

CONTINUED

6. The Jewel Room (Ephesians 4)

Notes:

7. The Choir and Oratory Room (Ephesians 5)

Notes:

8. The Armory (Ephesians 6)

Notes:

Before next session, read:
Sunday: Joy Triumphs over Suffering (Philippians 1:1-30)
Monday: Joy in Christ (Philippians 2:1-11)
Tuesday: Joy in Salvation (Philippians 2:12-30)
Wednesday: Joy in Christ's Righteousness (Philippians 3:1-9)
Thursday: Joy in Christ's Will (Philippians 3:10-21)
Friday: Joy in Christ's Strength (Philippians 4:1-7)
Saturday: Joy in Christ's Provision (Philippians 4:8-23)

THE FULL ARMOR OF GOD

Understanding Philippians

The purpose of this session is:

- To provide an overview of Paul's Epistle to the Philippians;
- To discover how Jesus Christ is revealed in Philippians as our Joy.

In this session, group members will learn:

- Key truths about God's story in Philippians;
- That Jesus is revealed as our source of Joy;
- The basic principle that sustaining our fellowship with Jesus Christ gives us strength and joy for living and for serving others in His name;
- How to apply the truths revealed in Philippians to their daily lives.

KEY VERSES

"Being confident of this, that he who began a good work in you will carry it on to completion until the day of Christ Jesus." Philippians 1:6

"For to me, to live is Christ and to die is gain." Philippians 1:21

"I want to know Christ and the power of his resurrection and the fellowship of sharing in his sufferings, become like him in his death, and so, somehow, to attain to the resurrection from the dead." Philippians 3:10,11

"Do not be anxious about anything, but in everything, by prayer and petition, with thanksgiving, present your requests to God. And the peace of God, which transcends all understanding, will guard your hearts and your minds in Christ Jesus." Philippians 4:6,7

"I can do everything through [Christ] who gives me strength." Philippians 4:13

"And my God will meet all your needs according to his glorious riches in Christ Jesus." Philippians 4:19

BEFORE THE SESSION

- Pray for group members by name, asking the Holy Spirit to reveal to them the spiritual truths in Philippians.

- Read chapter 37 in *What the Bible Is All About*.
- Prepare copies of Session 13 handout "God's Story in Philippians" for group members.
- Check off these supplies once you have secured them:
  - _____ A chalkboard and chalk or flip chart or overhead projector with markers.
  - _____ Extra Bibles, pencils and paper for group members.
  - _____ Three large sheets of poster board and felt-tip pens.
- If you are having a 90-minute session, carefully read the two option sections right now and pull together any supplies you need for them.
- Read the entire session and look up every passage. Have your Bible *Tuck-In*™ page ready.
- Arrive early and be ready to warmly greet each group member as he or she arrives.
- Memorize the key verses. Share them periodically and ask the group to repeat them as you teach the session.

SECTION ONE: GOD'S STORY (20 MINUTES)

GOD'S STORY IN PHILIPPIANS

Objective: To tell God's story so that Christians will apply the truths in Philippians to their own lives.

Greet everyone as they arrive. Tell the following story, doing the suggested activities as you come to them. Distribute the handout "God's Story in Philippians" to all group members.

The Letter of Joy

Paul's letter to Philippi was written to the first church founded in Europe (see Acts 16:12). As Paul wrote this letter in Rome, he was rejoicing while he was chained to a Roman soldier because he knew that those very chains helped him spread the gospel (see Philippians 1:12-30). The words "joy" and "rejoice" were used sixteen times in this letter. Obviously, Paul's joy was not derived from his circumstances but from an inner wellspring of joy in Jesus Christ (see 1:19,26).

Read Philippians 1:12-14, then discuss the following:
How did Paul's imprisonment help to spread the gospel?

How can the hardships we face become a motivation for sharing the gospel?

Joy in Living (Philippians 1)

Paul first of all rejoiced in his Philippian friends (see 1:3-5). Next he expressed his joy in the opportunity that prison afforded him to spread the gospel (see 1:12-29). His whole life and his thoughts of impending death were filled with joy because of his relationship and future with Christ (see 1:20-23).

Ask a volunteer to read John 16:22 out loud. Discuss:

Why do you believe Paul was able to hold onto joy in spite of imprisonment and facing death?

Paul's life theme is found in Philippians 1:18-21. How is such courage possible in living the Christian life?

Joy in Service (Philippians 2)

Paul instructed the Philippians to serve one another with the same attitude that Christ had as a servant (see 2:1-18).

Ask each group member to find a partner. Ask each pair to read the servant's hymn in Philippians 2:5-11 together and then have each partner choose one verse that means the most to him or her. Have them share the verse and why it is the most meaningful.

Joy in Fellowship (Philippians 3)

The sustaining fellowship with Jesus Christ is what gave Paul his strength and joy for living. His ambitions were not rooted in what he had accomplished in the world (see 3:7) but rather in how he might grow closer to Jesus (see 3:8-14).

Have group members carefully read Philippians 3:7-14 to themselves and then share what they discover about Paul's ambitions about knowing Christ. List the different ways Paul desired to know Jesus. Some of the ways might be:

> That I may gain Christ (3:8);
> That I may know Him (3:8,10);
> And be found in Him (3:9);
> That I may know the power of Christ's resurrection (3:10);
> That I may know the fellowship of sharing in His sufferings (3:10);
> That I may comprehend that for which also I am apprehended (3:12) (Paul desired to know Jesus' purposes for calling him to be an apostle);
> I press on toward the goal to win the prize for which God has called me heavenward in Christ Jesus (3:14).

Joy in Rewards (Philippians 4)

Paul rejoiced that the rewards of the Christian life were rooted in the Lord's return (see 4:4,5); the peace of God (see 4:7); the abiding presence of God (see 4:9);

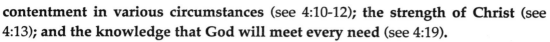

contentment in various circumstances (see 4:10-12); **the strength of Christ (see 4:13); and the knowledge that God will meet every need** (see 4:19).

Philippians 4 is one of the greatest chapters in the Bible. Ask group members to find their favorite verse in chapter 4 and share why it is a favorite.

OPTION ONE: (FOR A 90-MINUTE SESSION)

Have No Anxiety (15 Minutes)

Ask everyone to list on paper all the things in life that make them anxious. Some of the things they mention might include:

> **financial problems;**
> **spiritual attacks on my children;**
> **physical illness;**
> **emotional stress;**
> **rejection by someone I care about.**

Have everyone follow along in their Bibles as you read Philippians 4:6,7 out loud, then discuss:

How should you handle anxiety as a Christian?

How do you conquer fear?

Have everyone find a partner, then discuss and pray with one another about the anxieties they need to surrender to Christ.

SECTION TWO: GOD'S PERSON (15 MINUTES)

THE CHRISTIAN: HAVING THE JOY OF THE LORD AND THE MIND OF CHRIST

Objective: To discover the reality and depth of living the Christian life filled with His joy.

The joyful Christian has the mind of Christ (see 1 Corinthians 2:16). What does it mean to "have the mind of Christ"?

Divide the group into three groups. Give each group a large sheet of poster board and some felt-tip pens. Ask each group to draw a picture representing what they understand the mind of Christ to be, based on Philippians 2:5-11 and 4:8,9. Give the groups about seven minutes to complete their posters and then have each group share their poster with the whole group.

Discuss:

Why should serving others be a joy and not a duty for the Christian?
How can we keep our minds fixed on what is excellent?

OPTION TWO: (FOR A 90-MINUTE SESSION)

The Secret of Contentment (15 Minutes)

Many of us search for happiness instead of joy. Happiness is temporary because it is tied to our circumstances. Whatever happens to us determines how we feel. On the other hand, joy is rooted in Jesus Christ—who is "the same yesterday and today and forever" (Hebrews 13:8). Paul revealed the secret to contentment in Philippians 4:10-13.

Have the group form pairs and share their completions to the sentences in the handout section entitled "Happiness or Joy?". Then have them share with one another how the world or Satan tries to rob us of our joy. Finally invite them to pray for one another to be content in Christ no matter what the circumstance.

SECTION THREE: GOD'S SON (15 MINUTES)

JESUS CHRIST REVEALED AS OUR JOY

Objective: To see how Jesus is revealed as our source of joy and strength as we face every circumstance in life, including the trials and difficulties.

Ask everyone to turn to Philippians 4:13,19. Write the verses on the board, flip chart or overhead one word or phrase at a time in the following manner:

> **I can do...**
> **everything...**
> **through [Christ]...**
> **who gives me strength.**
> **And my God...**
> **will meet all [my] needs...**
> **according to his glorious riches...**
> **in Christ Jesus.**

Have group members write the phrases down on the back of their handouts and meditate on each phrase for one minute, saying them over and over again in their minds. Then have them share which phrase the Holy Spirit is most strongly speaking to their hearts and what they rejoice in hearing Him say through this phrase.

PURSUING GOD (5 MINUTES)

NEXT STEPS I NEED TO TAKE

Objective: To take a realistic assessment of one's relationship with Jesus and how that relationship might grow closer in the coming week.

Have them find their partners again. Ask each pair to share their completions to the following statements:

One way I need to become more of a servant like Jesus is...

One step I need to take to rely more on Jesus as my source of joy is ...

One attitude from Philippians 4:8 that needs to grow in my life is...

PRAYER (5 MINUTES)

Objective: To pray out of Christ's joy from within us.

Have the group form a circle. Pray sentence prayers around the circle, expressing their joy for something that the Lord is teaching them or doing in their lives.

Session 13 Bible *Tuck-In*™

UNDERSTANDING PHILIPPIANS

The purpose of this session is:

- To provide an overview of Paul's Epistle to the Philippians;
- To discover how Jesus Christ is revealed in Philippians as our joy.

KEY VERSES

"Being confident of this, that he who began a good work in you will carry it on to completion until the day of Christ Jesus." Philippians 1:6

"For to me, to live is Christ and to die is gain." Philippians 1:21

"I want to know Christ and the power of his resurrection and the fellowship of sharing in his sufferings, become like him in his death, and so, somehow, to attain to the resurrection from the dead." Philippians 3:10,11

"Do not be anxious about anything, but in everything, by prayer and petition, with thanksgiving, present your requests to God. And the peace of God, which transcends all understanding, will guard your hearts and your minds in Christ Jesus." Philippians 4:6,7

---

through [Christ]...
who gives me strength.
And my God...
will meet all [my] needs...
according to his glorious riches...
in Christ Jesus.

- Have group members write the phrases down on the back of their handouts and meditate on each phrase for one minute, saying them over and over again in their minds. Then have them share which phrase the Holy Spirit is most strongly speaking to their hearts and what they rejoice in hearing Him say through this phrase.

PURSUING GOD (5 MINUTES)

NEXT STEPS I NEED TO TAKE

- Have them find their partners again. Ask each pair to share their completions to the following statements:

One way I need to become more of a servant like Jesus is...

One step I need to take to rely more on Jesus as my source of joy is ...

One attitude from Philippians 4:8 that needs to grow in my life is...

PRAYER (5 MINUTES)

- Have the group form a circle. Pray sentence prayers around the circle, expressing their joy for something that the Lord is teaching them or doing in their lives.

"I can do everything through [Christ] who gives me strength." Philippians 4:13

"And my God will meet all your needs according to his glorious riches in Christ Jesus." Philippians 4:19

SECTION ONE: GOD'S STORY (20 MINUTES)

GOD'S STORY IN PHILIPPIANS

- Greet everyone as they arrive. Tell the story of Philippians, doing the suggested activities as you come to them. Distribute the handout "God's Story in Philippians" to all group members.

OPTION ONE: (FOR A 90-MINUTE SESSION)

Have No Anxiety (15 Minutes)

- Ask everyone to list on paper all the things in life that make them anxious. Some of the things they mention might include: **financial problems; worldly attacks on my children such as drugs, sexual temptations and violence; physical illness; emotional stress; rejection by someone I care about.**

- Have everyone follow along in their Bibles as you read Philippians 4:6,7 aloud. Then discuss:

  How should you handle anxiety as a Christian?

  How do you conquer fear?

- Have everyone find a partner, then discuss and pray with one another about the anxieties they need to surrender to Christ.

-------- Fold --------

SECTION TWO: GOD'S PERSON (15 MINUTES)

THE CHRISTIAN: HAVING THE JOY OF THE LORD AND THE MIND OF CHRIST

- Divide the group into three groups. Give each group a large sheet of poster board and some felt-tip pens. Ask each group to draw a picture representing what they understand the mind of Christ to be, based on Philippians 2:5-11 and 4:8,9. Give the groups about seven minutes to complete their posters and then have each group share their poster with the whole group. Discuss:

  How should serving others be a joy and not a duty for the Christian?

  How can we keep our minds fixed on what is excellent?

OPTION TWO: (FOR A 90-MINUTE SESSION)

The Secret of Contentment (15 Minutes)

- Have the group form pairs and share their completions to the sentences in the handout section entitled "Happiness or Joy?" Then have them share with one another how the world or Satan tries to rob us of our joy. Finally invite them to pray for one another to be content in Christ no matter what the circumstance.

SECTION THREE: GOD'S SON (15 MINUTES)

JESUS CHRIST REVEALED AS OUR JOY

- Ask everyone to turn to Philippians 4:13,19. Write the verses on the board, flip chart or overhead one word or phrase at a time in the following manner:

  I can do…

  everything…

GOD'S STORY IN PHILIPPIANS

1. The Letter of Joy

   Notes:

2. Joy in Living (Philippians 1)

   Notes:

3. Joy in Service (Philippians 2)

   Notes:

4. Joy in Fellowship (Philippians 3)

   Notes:

HAPPINESS OR JOY?

Beside each item, write *H* for happiness or *J* for joy if that particular item brings you temporary happiness or lasting joy.

_____ 1. Leading someone to Jesus as Lord and Savior.

_____ 2. Knowing Jesus personally as my Lord and Savior.

_____ 3. Being financially successful.

_____ 4. Having a nice home.

_____ 5. Achieving status among my peers.

CONTINUED

    _____ 6. Being loved by my family.

    _____ 7. Worshiping God.

    _____ 8. Having sufficient food and clothing.

5. Joy in Rewards (Philippians 4)

Notes:

Before next session, read:
Sunday: Paul's Greeting and Prayer (Colossians 1:1-14)
Monday: Seven Superiorities of Christ (Colossians 1:15-29)
Tuesday: Christ Exalted (Colossians 2:1-16)
Wednesday: Complete in Christ (Colossians 2:1-19)
Thursday: Old and New Man (Colossians 2:20—3:11)
Friday: Christian Living (Colossians 3:12-25)
Saturday: Christian Graces (Colossians 4:1-18)

Bible Study Plans
Leader Instructions

As leader, photocopy the following Study Plan pages to distribute to your group. Copy the pages in duplex format so they can be easily inserted inside a Bible. Group members have the option of following a one-year plan or a two-year plan.

When you introduce the Study Plan to your group, refer to the information on the "Introduction to Study Chart" page to stimulate interest and communicate the value of this Bible Study Plan. If you have never completed such a plan yourself, join the group in committing to follow through on the monthly readings.

Should much of the current month already be gone, instruct them to simply make the "First Month" on the chart include the rest of this month and next month. Also, if there are any months in the year (e.g., December) when a person knows his or her schedule may not allow time for continuing the study plan, suggest that month be left off the chart and the name of the following month written in its place. During that "vacation" month a person may select one or more favorite sections of Scripture (e.g., Psalms, Proverbs, 1 John) in which to do devotional reading until the schedule is back to normal and the study plan can resume. It is better to plan on taking an extra month or two to complete the study than to get discouraged and quit should reading fall behind.

NOTE: If some people have doubts that they will successfully complete the Bible Study Plan, share a few tips to help them keep going should their determination waver:

1. Tell a friend what you are setting out to do and ask him or her to pray for you and regularly check with you on your progress. Making yourself accountable to someone else will help you maintain your pace and help you apply what you learn.

2. Enlist a friend to join you in the plan. Meeting together regularly to talk and to pray about what you have learned is both beneficial and motivational. Ask God to help you apply one principle you read about each day to your walk with Him.

3. Promise yourself some rewards for completing stages of the plan. You may enjoy anticipating a favorite treat each time you complete a suggested reading goal or all the suggested reading for a month. Also, think of some-

thing special to do at the end of three months or six months or the full year. For example, why not plan a "celebration" to which you will invite a few close friends? Invite them out for dinner or dessert and include a brief explanation of some of the benefits you have gained from your Bible reading and prayer.

4. Pray regularly, telling God your doubts about "sticking it out." Ask Him for help in sticking with the daily readings and for help in understanding how He wants you to apply His Word to your life.

Bible Study Plan
Introduction to
Study Chart

As valuable as a group study is, there is no substitute for systematic, personal Bible study and prayer to grow in your walk with Christ. The plan outlined here will make Bible reading spiritually enriching as well as help deepen your understanding of the Bible both as the history of God's people and as the remarkable unified Book of God's Plan for all humanity. By following this plan, you can read through the Bible in a year, using the helpful guidance contained in *What the Bible Is All About*.

Some people become discouraged in reading the Bible from beginning to end. Some Old Testament sections are difficult to understand and even more difficult to apply to life today. Therefore, this plan lets you spend time each month in three different sections of the Bible: Old Testament Law and History, Old Testament Poetry and Prophecy, and the New Testament. The monthly Bible passages are of similar length rather than trying to complete a book by an arbitrary date. Thus, some pages in *What the Bible Is All About* are listed as resources in more than one month.

This study plan is flexible, giving you some structure and goals but allowing you to study in the way that fits you best, perhaps even varying your approach throughout the year. For example:

- Rather than giving daily assignments that may be burdensome, this plan gives monthly guidelines, letting you set the pace.
- You may prefer to set aside time every day for Bible study. Or you might enjoy reading in longer time blocks several times a week.
- You might favor the variety that comes by reading from each of the three main sections at each study session. Or you may elect to complete the month's study of each section separately.
- You might want to read the recommended sections of *What the Bible Is All About* before starting to read the Bible portions. Or you may choose to read the Bible first and then use *What the Bible Is All About* to help you understand what you have read.
- You can decide when to start your study. Keep the chart on the following pages in your Bible or in your copy of *What the Bible Is All About*. As you complete a month's suggested reading, mark the reference on the chart as an indication of your progress.

One-Year Bible Study Plan

What the Bible Is All About Chart

First Month:

Old Testament: Law and History
Genesis 1—37 _____   *WTBIAA* pp. 13-40 _____
Old Testament: Poetry and Prophecy
Job 1—42 _____   *WTBIAA* pp. 173-185 _____
New Testament
Matthew 1—20 _____   *WTBIAA* pp. 337-357 _____

Second Month:

Old Testament: Law and History
Genesis 38—Exodus 25 _____ *WTBIAA* pp. 40-49 _____
Old Testament: Poetry and Prophecy
Psalm 1—62 _____   *WTBIAA* pp. 187-191 _____
New Testament
Matthew 21—Mark 8 _____   *WTBIAA* pp. 357-371 _____

Third Month:

Old Testament: Law and History
Exodus 26—Leviticus 23 _____ WTBIAA pp. 49-59 _____
Old Testament: Poetry and Prophecy
Psalm 63—117 _____   *WTBIAA* pp. 191-193 _____
New Testament
Mark 9—Luke 6 _____   *WTBIAA* pp. 371-387 _____

Fourth Month:

Old Testament: Law and History
Leviticus 24—Numbers 28 _____ *WTBIAA* pp. 59-71 _____
Old Testament: Poetry and Prophecy
Psalm 118—Proverbs 18 _____ *WTBIAA* pp. 193-199 _____
New Testament
Luke 7—22 _____   *WTBIAA* pp. 387-391 _____

FIFTH MONTH:

Old Testament: Law and History
Numbers 29—Deuteronomy 30 _____ *WTBIAA* pp. 71-78 _____
Old Testament: Poetry and Prophecy
Proverbs 19—Isaiah 8 _____ *WTBIAA* pp. 199-217 _____
New Testament
Luke 23—John 13 _____ *WTBIAA* pp. 391-406 _____

SIXTH MONTH:

Old Testament: Law and History
Deuteronomy 31—Judges 8 _____ *WTBIAA* pp. 78-106 _____
Old Testament: Poetry and Prophecy
Isaiah 9—43 _____ *WTBIAA* pp. 217-221 _____
New Testament
John 14—Acts 11 _____ *WTBIAA* pp. 406-422 _____

SEVENTH MONTH:

Old Testament: Law and History
Judges 9—1 Samuel 21 _____ *WTBIAA* pp. 106-118 _____
Old Testament: Poetry and Prophecy
Isaiah 44—Jeremiah 6 _____ *WTBIAA* pp. 221-229 _____
New Testament
Acts 12—Romans 1 _____ *WTBIAA* pp. 422-434 _____

EIGHTH MONTH:

Old Testament: Law and History
1 Samuel 22—1 Kings 2 _____ *WTBIAA* pp. 118-136 _____
Old Testament: Poetry and Prophecy
Jeremiah 7—38 _____ *WTBIAA* pp. 229-234 _____
New Testament
Romans 2—1 Corinthians 11 _____ *WTBIAA* pp. 434-453 _____

NINTH MONTH:

Old Testament: Law and History
1 Kings 3—2 Kings 10 _____ *WTBIAA* pp. 136-143 _____
Old Testament: Poetry and Prophecy
Jeremiah 39—Ezekiel 15 _____ *WTBIAA* pp. 234-250 _____
New Testament
1 Corinthians 12—Ephesians 6 _____ *WTBIAA* pp. 453-490 _____

TENTH MONTH:

Old Testament: Law and History
2 Kings 11—1 Chronicles 17 _____   *WTBIAA* pp. 143-145 _____
Old Testament: Poetry and Prophecy
Ezekiel 16—45 _____   *WTBIAA* pp. 250-253 _____
New Testament
Philippians 1—Philemon _____   *WTBIAA* pp. 491-559 _____

ELEVENTH MONTH:

Old Testament: Law and History
1 Chronicles 18—2 Chronicles 31 _____   *WTBIAA* pp. 145-146 _____
Old Testament: Poetry and Prophecy
Ezekiel 46—Amos 9 _____   *WTBIAA* pp. 253-292 _____
New Testament
Hebrews 1—2 Peter 3 _____   *WTBIAA* pp. 561-607 _____

TWELFTH MONTH:

Old Testament: Law and History
2 Chronicles 32—Esther 10 _____   *WTBIAA* pp. 146-171 _____
Old Testament: Poetry and Prophecy
Obadiah 1—Malachi 4 _____   *WTBIAA* pp. 293-334 _____
New Testament
1 John 1—Revelation 22 _____   *WTBIAA* pp. 609-636 _____

Two-Year
Bible Study Plan
What the Bible Is All About Chart

FIRST MONTH:

Old Testament: Law and History
Genesis 1—21 _____   *WTBIAA* pp. 13-40 _____
Old Testament: Poetry and Prophecy
Job 1—20 _____   *WTBIAA* pp. 173-182 _____
New Testament
Matthew 1—11 _____   *WTBIAA* pp. 337-353 _____

SECOND MONTH:

Old Testament: Law and History
Genesis 22—37 _____   *WTBIAA* p. 40 _____
Old Testament: Poetry and Prophecy
Job 21—42 _____   *WTBIAA* pp. 182-185 _____
New Testament
Matthew 12—20 _____   *WTBIAA* pp. 353-357 _____

THIRD MONTH:

Old Testament: Law and History
Genesis 38—Exodus 6 _____   *WTBIAA* pp. 40-45 _____
Old Testament: Poetry and Prophecy
Psalm 1—33 _____   *WTBIAA* pp. 187-189 _____
New Testament
Matthew 21—27 _____   *WTBIAA* pp. 357-360 _____

FOURTH MONTH:

Old Testament: Law and History
Exodus 7—25 _____   *WTBIAA* pp. 45-49 _____
Old Testament: Poetry and Prophecy
Psalm 34—66 _____   *WTBIAA* pp. 189-191 _____
New Testament
Matthew 28—Mark 8 _____   *WTBIAA* pp. 360-376 _____

FIFTH MONTH:

Old Testament: Law and History
Exodus 26—Leviticus 5 _____ *WTBIAA* pp. 49-52 _____
Old Testament: Poetry and Prophecy
Psalm 67—88 _____ *WTBIAA* pp. 191-192 _____
New Testament
Mark 9—16 _____ *WTBIAA* pp. 376-380 _____

SIXTH MONTH:

Old Testament: Law and History
Leviticus 6—23 _____ *WTBIAA* pp. 52-57 _____
Old Testament: Poetry and Prophecy
Psalm 89—117 _____ *WTBIAA* pp. 192-193 _____
New Testament
Luke 1—6 _____ *WTBIAA* pp. 381-387 _____

SEVENTH MONTH:

Old Testament: Law and History
Leviticus 24—Numbers 11 _____ *WTBIAA* pp. 57-65 _____
Old Testament: Poetry and Prophecy
Psalm 118—150 _____ *WTBIAA* pp. 193-194 _____
New Testament
Luke 7—13 _____ *WTBIAA* p. 387 _____

EIGHTH MONTH:

Old Testament: Law and History
Numbers 12—28 _____ *WTBIAA* pp. 65-71 _____
Old Testament: Poetry and Prophecy
Proverbs 1—18 _____ *WTBIAA* pp. 195-199 _____
New Testament
Luke 14—23 _____ *WTBIAA* pp. 387-392 _____

NINTH MONTH:

Old Testament: Law and History
Numbers 29—Deuteronomy 9 _____ *WTBIAA* pp. 71-77 _____
Old Testament: Poetry and Prophecy
Proverbs 19—Ecclesiastes 7 _____ *WTBIAA* pp. 199-202 _____
New Testament
Luke 24—John 6 _____ *WTBIAA* pp. 392-403 _____

TENTH MONTH:
Old Testament: Law and History
Deuteronomy 10—30 _____   *WTBIAA* pp. 77-78 _____
Old Testament: Poetry and Prophecy
Ecclesiastes 8—Isaiah 8 _____   *WTBIAA* pp. 202-217 _____
New Testament
John 7—13 _____   *WTBIAA* pp. 403-406 _____

ELEVENTH MONTH:
Old Testament: Law and History
Deuteronomy 31—Joshua 14 _____   *WTBIAA* pp. 78-91 _____
Old Testament: Poetry and Prophecy
Isaiah 9—27 _____   *WTBIAA* pp. 217-219 _____
New Testament
John 14—Acts 2 _____   *WTBIAA* pp. 406-418 _____

TWELFTH MONTH:
Old Testament: Law and History
Joshua 15—Judges 8 _____   *WTBIAA* pp. 91-101 _____
Old Testament: Poetry and Prophecy
Isaiah 28—43 _____   *WTBIAA* pp. 219-221 _____
New Testament
Acts 3—11 _____   *WTBIAA* pp. 418-422 _____

THIRTEENTH MONTH:
Old Testament: Law and History
Judges 9—1 Samuel 2 _____   *WTBIAA* pp. 101-112 _____
Old Testament: Poetry and Prophecy
Isaiah 44—59 _____   *WTBIAA* p. 221 _____
New Testament
Acts 12—20 _____   *WTBIAA* pp. 422-425 _____

FOURTEENTH MONTH:
Old Testament: Law and History
1 Samuel 3—21 _____   *WTBIAA* pp. 112-118 _____
Old Testament: Poetry and Prophecy
Isaiah 60—Jeremiah 6 _____   *WTBIAA* pp. 221-229 _____
New Testament
Acts 21—Romans 1 _____   *WTBIAA* pp. 425-434 _____

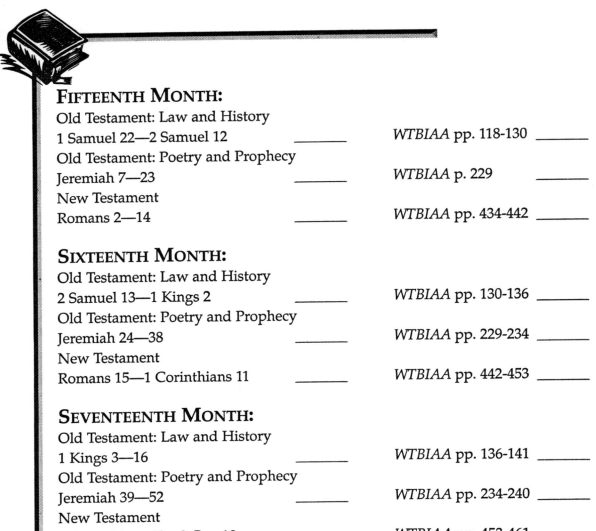

FIFTEENTH MONTH:
Old Testament: Law and History
1 Samuel 22—2 Samuel 12 _____   *WTBIAA* pp. 118-130 _____
Old Testament: Poetry and Prophecy
Jeremiah 7—23 _____   *WTBIAA* p. 229 _____
New Testament
Romans 2—14 _____   *WTBIAA* pp. 434-442 _____

SIXTEENTH MONTH:
Old Testament: Law and History
2 Samuel 13—1 Kings 2 _____   *WTBIAA* pp. 130-136 _____
Old Testament: Poetry and Prophecy
Jeremiah 24—38 _____   *WTBIAA* pp. 229-234 _____
New Testament
Romans 15—1 Corinthians 11 _____   *WTBIAA* pp. 442-453 _____

SEVENTEENTH MONTH:
Old Testament: Law and History
1 Kings 3—16 _____   *WTBIAA* pp. 136-141 _____
Old Testament: Poetry and Prophecy
Jeremiah 39—52 _____   *WTBIAA* pp. 234-240 _____
New Testament
1 Corinthians 12—2 Cor. 10 _____   *WTBIAA* pp. 453-461 _____

EIGHTEENTH MONTH:
Old Testament: Law and History
1 Kings 17—2 Kings 10 _____   *WTBIAA* pp. 142-143 _____
Old Testament: Poetry and Prophecy
Lamentations 1—Ezekiel 15 _____   *WTBIAA* pp. 240-250 _____
New Testament
2 Corinthians 11—Ephesians 6 _____   *WTBIAA* pp. 461-490 _____

NINETEENTH MONTH:
Old Testament: Law and History
2 Kings 11—1 Chronicles 1 _____   *WTBIAA* pp. 143-145 _____
Old Testament: Poetry and Prophecy
Ezekiel 16—29 _____   *WTBIAA* pp. 250-253 _____
New Testament
Philippians 1—1 Thessalonians 5 _____   *WTBIAA* pp. 491-523 _____

Twentieth Month:

Old Testament: Law and History
1 Chronicles 2—17 _____ *WTBIAA* pp. 145-146 _____
Old Testament: Poetry and Prophecy
Ezekiel 30—45 _____ *WTBIAA* p. 253 _____
New Testament
2 Thessalonians 1—Philemon _____ *WTBIAA* pp. 525-559 _____

Twenty-first Month:

Old Testament: Law and History
1 Chronicles 18—2 Chronicles 8 _____ *WTBIAA* pp. 145-146 _____
Old Testament: Poetry and Prophecy
Ezekiel 46—Daniel 12 _____ *WTBIAA* pp. 253-272 _____
New Testament
Hebrews 1—13 _____ *WTBIAA* pp. 561-571 _____

Twenty-second Month:

Old Testament: Law and History
2 Chronicles 9—31 _____ *WTBIAA* p. 146 _____
Old Testament: Poetry and Prophecy
Hosea 1—Amos 6 _____ *WTBIAA* pp. 273-290 _____
New Testament
James 1—2 Peter 3 _____ *WTBIAA* pp. 573-607 _____

Twenty-third Month:

Old Testament: Law and History
2 Chronicles 32—Nehemiah 3 _____ *WTBIAA* pp. 146-153 _____
Old Testament: Poetry and Prophecy
Amos 7—Habakkuk 3 _____ *WTBIAA* pp. 290-314 _____
New Testament
1 John 1—Revelation 8 _____ *WTBIAA* pp. 609-628 _____

Twenty-fourth Month:

Old Testament: Law and History
Nehemiah 4—Esther 10 _____ *WTBIAA* pp. 153-171 _____
Old Testament: Poetry and Prophecy
Zephaniah 1—Malachi 4 _____ *WTBIAA* pp. 314-334 _____
New Testament
Revelation 9—22 _____ *WTBIAA* pp. 628-636 _____

CERTIFICATE OF COMPLETION

This is to certify that

_____

Name

has completed the course, *What the Bible Is All About 201 New Testament: Matthew—Philippians*

on this day _____

_____

Signed

Continue Your Adventure in God's Word

What the Bible Is All About™ is one of the all-time favorite Bible handbooks. This classic 4-million copy best-seller and its family of resources will help you stamp out biblical illiteracy.

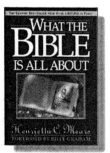

What the Bible Is All About™
Henrietta C. Mears

The classic 4-million-copy-best-seller takes the reader on a personal journey through the entire Bible, covering the basics in a simple, understandable way.

Hardcover • ISBN 08307.16084
Paperback • ISBN 08307.16076

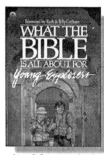

What the Bible Is All About™ for Young Explorers
Frances Blankenbaker

The basics of **What the Bible Is All About**,™ in a graphic visual format designed to make the Bible more approachable for youth.

Hardcover • ISBN 08307.11791
Paperback • ISBN 08307.11627

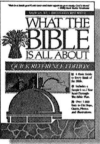

What the Bible Is All About™ Quick-Reference Edition

This easy-to-use Bible handbook gives a brief overview of the people, events and meaning of every book of the Bible. Includes over 1,000 illustrations, charts and time lines.

Hardcover • ISBN 08307.13905
Paperback • ISBN 08307.18486

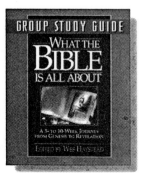

What the Bible Is All About™ Group Study Guide
Wes Haystead

A teaching companion for the best selling classic. In 5 to 10 weeks you will give your students an overview of the Bible with concrete illustrations and clear commentary.
Includes reproducible study sheets.

Group Study Guide • ISBN 08307.16009

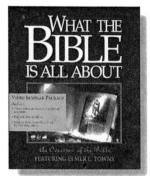

What the Bible Is All About Video Seminar
Elmer L. Towns

Here, in just three hours, Dr. Elmer Towns presents an outline of God's plan for the ages. He shows how this plan is established on six key "turning points" in history. Armed with a clear understanding of these foundation points, students can turn to the Bible with a deeper understanding of its content.

Video Seminar • SPCN 85116.00906
(Package includes book, reproducible syllabus and 2 video tapes.)
Audio tapes • ISBN 75116.00611

Gospel Light
These resources are available at your local Christian bookstore.

New! What the Bible Is All About™ Group Study Guides!

Teach through the Bible in one year with these 13-session studies laying out the Bible in an understandable, tangible way, giving students a panoramic, big-picture view of God's love and plan for His children.

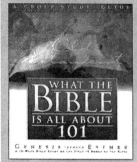

What the Bible Is All About™ 101 Group Study Guide Old Testament: Genesis-Esther
Henrietta Mears

Here's a 13-session study that takes your class through some of the most important—and yet least understood—books of the Bible. Students will also get a clear picture of Jesus as He is revealed throughout the Old Testament.

Manual • ISBN 08307.17951

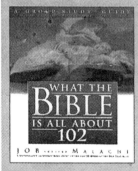

What the Bible Is All About™ 102 Group Study Guide Old Testament: Job-Malachi
Henrietta Mears

Introduce your students to the poetry and prophecy of the Old Testament—and what it teaches us about God's plan for all time–fulfilled in Jesus Christ.

Manual • ISBN 08307.17978

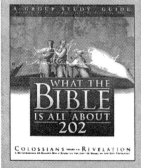

What the Bible Is All About™ 202 Group Study Guide New Testament: Colossians-Revelation
Henrietta Mears

As you take your class through the last 16 books of the Bible they'll see how all of the scriptures are woven together by God into a beautiful tapestry that tells about His plan for all time.

Manual • ISBN 08307.17994

Teach the Whole Bible at a Fraction of the Price

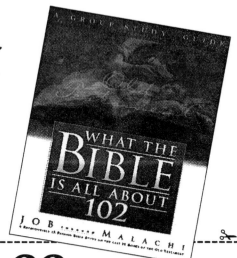

Continue your journey through the Bible and save some money along the way.

Here's a coupon for $2.00 off your purchase of the **What the Bible Is All About 102 Old Testament: Job—Malachi Group Study Guide!** There are 4 books in the entire series, so be on the look-out for your coupon as you begin your New Testament studies next quarter!

You've made it half way through the Old Testament, here's an incentive to help you make it all the way through.

Look for the other volumes of the *What the Bible Is All About 101* series:

**What the Bible Is All About 102
Old Testament:
Job—Malachi Group Study Guide**

**What the Bible Is All About 201
New Testament:
Matthew—Philippians Group Study Guide**

**What the Bible Is All About 202
New Testament:
Colossians—Revelation Group Study Guide**